I AM JESUS
The Resurrection

Karen Mitchell

Dedication

I would like to thank my Great God—the Father, Son, and Holy Spirit! I dedicate and consecrate myself wholly to Him, and I attribute every good thing in my life to God; without Him, I am unable to do anything.

I dedicate this book to my children, Anthony Mitchell, Christina Mitchell Paris, Delana Mitchell, Tonnette, and Shawn, who have supported me throughout the writing process in so many ways.

I also dedicate this book to the memory of my late husband, Francis Anthony Mitchell, and my two daughters, Lauren and Briona Mitchell. Additionally, I would like to honor my mother, Betty; my father, Norris; my grandmother, Leola; and my brother, Keith. They will always remain in my thoughts.

I also pray for all those who have died with hope in the faith of the Resurrection, believing in Jesus and His word. May the Lord God reveal Himself to those who do not yet believe on their journey here in time, so they may live in eternity, united with God through Christ Jesus.

Contents

Introduction

Life is a journey of self-discovery, a path where we seek to understand who we are and where we come from. In this quest, there is a singular, profound starting point that offers answers unavailable elsewhere. These answers do more than illuminate our existence; they provide a deep understanding of why it is essential to know Jesus.

In His boundless wisdom and love, the Almighty God has left humanity a remarkable heritage, a spiritual genealogy that goes beyond the parameters of physical tests or DNA analysis. Through embracing Jesus Christ and His completed work on the Cross, an individual experiences a rebirth of sorts. This rebirth is not of flesh but of spirit, bringing one into the vast, loving family of God.

In this family, there are no strangers, only brothers and sisters united under the grace of God. Here, in this divine kinship, we find our true identity. It is not just about discovering our earthly selves but realizing our eternal role in God's grand design. This realization is not an endpoint but a beginning—the start of a journey where we walk in the light of Christ, learning and growing in His love each day.

As we delve into this narrative, our starting point will be an exploration of this spiritual lineage and its deep implications. We will explore how knowing Jesus reshapes our understanding of life, existence, and our place in the universe. The journey with Christ is one of transformation, where the old self fades away, and a new, spiritually awakened self emerges, ready to embrace the fullness of life in God's eternal family.

To fully grasp man's genealogy, we need to travel back to the beginning, to the roots of our identity. This identity, in its most authentic form, is discovered in Jesus. Whether you are familiar with Jesus or just beginning to learn about Him, the insights in this book will guide you on a journey of self-discovery. It's akin to the journey of an adopted child seeking to know their biological parents. Just as that child yearns to understand their origins, we, too, have a deep-seated desire to connect with our spiritual origin.

In this physical world, we are born to human parents. They nurture us, teach us, and help shape our early understanding of life. Yet, beyond this physical existence, there is a higher truth. In our truest sense, we are the creations of the one true God. He is our ultimate Creator, the originator of our being.

Understanding this connection with God through Jesus is like uncovering a hidden treasure that has always been ours. It's a realization that we are more than just physical beings; we are spiritual entities with a divine heritage. This book aims to bridge that gap between our earthly existence and our heavenly lineage. It seeks to reveal how our identity in Jesus connects us to God, offering a sense of belonging, purpose, and eternal love that transcends our worldly experience.

This exploration into your true self is crucial for comprehending your nature, innate gifts, and life's purpose. Every reader of this book is distinctly blessed with a unique role to play in this vast universe. In this journey to discover Jesus, you will not only affirm your identity but also gain clarity on the individual path that God has lovingly laid out for you.

God, in His infinite wisdom and grace, does not impose this purpose upon you. Rather, He gently reveals it, weaving it through your desires, talents, and gifts. This process is not forceful but rather a natural unfolding of your inherent potential. As you align yourself with God's vision, your true purpose becomes increasingly clear, harmoniously blending your personal aspirations with His plan.

Embracing this purpose does more than fulfill you as an individual; it glorifies God. It's a testament to His magnificent design, where each life is a unique, irreplaceable thread in the complex interweave of creation. When you live out your God-given purpose, you find personal satisfaction and contribute to the greater glory of the Almighty.

So, together, let us embark on this journey of self-realization together. It's a path of discovery, growth, and spiritual awakening. Together, we will uncover the deepest truths about who we are, our connection to Jesus, and our role in God's grand narrative. It's a journey of understanding and transformation, where each step brings us closer to our truest selves and our calling. Let us begin this journey now with open hearts and eager spirits, ready to embrace the fullness of our identity in Christ.

Chapter 1: I Am Who I Am

In the beginning God created the heavens and the earth. Now the earth was formless and empty, darkness was over the surface of the deep, and the Spirit of God was hovering over the waters.

And God said, "Let there be light," and there was light. God saw that the light was good, and he separated the light from the darkness. God called the light "day," and the darkness he called "night." And there was evening, and there was morning—the first day.

-Genesis 1:1-5

As we delve into the remarkable event of Jesus' Resurrection, we are drawn into an encounter with the sincerest form of love ever known to mankind. This chapter, aptly titled "I Am Who I Am," is not just a statement about God but also a mirror reflecting our true selves.

In examining Jesus's life and resurrection, we see Him not only as a mirror reflecting our current state but also as a guide showing us who we are meant to become. Jesus, in His life, death, and resurrection, embodies the perfect image of what humanity can aspire to. He is the embodiment of love, grace, and truth.

Jesus' identity as "I Am" is deeply intertwined with our own identity. In Him, we find the answers to our deepest questions about who we are and what we are meant to be. His life serves as a blueprint, a divine example of living in harmony with God's will.

As we journey through this chapter, we will explore how Jesus' resurrection is a cornerstone of the Christian faith and a pivotal moment that redefines our understanding of self. It reveals to us the immense potential and purpose we carry within us as children of God.

In Exodus 3:14-15, we find a moment of thoughtful revelation. God speaks to Moses from the burning bush, revealing His name as "I AM WHO I AM." This declaration is not just a name but a declaration to God's eternal, self-existent nature. He is the beginning and the end, the all-encompassing One. When God instructs Moses to tell the children of Israel that "I AM has sent me to you," He is establishing a foundation for understanding His unchanging and everlasting nature.

This passage is pivotal for several reasons. First, it connects us to the heritage of faith. God identifies Himself as the God of Abraham, Isaac, and Jacob, linking Moses and the Israelites to their ancestors' covenant with God. This continuity shows that God's presence and promises are steadfast through generations.

Secondly, the name "I AM" reveals God's omnipresence and omnipotence. He is not a deity confined by time, space, or human limitations. This understanding of God is essential as we explore the life and resurrection of Jesus. In Jesus, we see the embodiment of "I AM" - the eternal presence of God made manifest in human form. Jesus is the bridge between the divine and the human, showing us the perfect blend of humanity touched by the divine.

Reflecting on this truth allows us to grasp the depth of what it means to be created in God's image. Just as God is "I AM," there is an aspect of this identity within each of us. We are not just fleeting, temporal beings; we carry within us the imprint of the eternal, the image of the "I AM." This is not to say we are divine like God is, but rather that our true identity is rooted in something far greater than our earthly existence.

In comprehending this, we begin to understand our worth, purpose, and potential. Our lives are not just a series of random events; they are part of a divine narrative woven by the hands of the "I AM." This revelation is empowering and humbling, as it calls us to live in a way that reflects our divine origin and destiny.

In Exodus chapter 6, we encounter another profound aspect of God's identity: His name is written as YHWH, often referred to as the Tetragrammaton. This four-letter Hebrew name, יְהֹוָה, is a sacred reference to God, so revered and holy that in Jewish tradition, it is traditionally not pronounced aloud. Instead, other names like Adonai (Lord) or Elohim (God) are used in its place. The letters of this divine name, read from right to left in Hebrew, are Yodh, He, Waw, and He.

This deep respect for the name of God underlines its sacredness and the reverence with which God's presence and identity are treated in the Jewish faith. It's a recognition of the holiness and majesty of God, an acknowledgment that there is something about the divine nature that is beyond human comprehension and articulation.

In Christianity, various names and titles are used to refer to God. Some have used Jehovah, a Latinization of the Tetragrammaton, while others refer to Him as Adonai, Elohim, or

Hashem. These different names and titles reflect the diverse ways people have tried to understand and relate to the divine.

Significantly, in the New Testament, Jesus is associated with these divine names and titles. This association is not just nominal; it signifies a deep theological truth about Jesus' identity and nature. Jesus is not just a historical figure; He embodies the presence of God, the "I AM," among us. His life and teachings provide a tangible connection to the divine, offering a new way to understand and experience God's presence.

As we analyze these divine names and their connection to Jesus, we gain a richer understanding of the nature of God and our relationship with Him. It helps us see Jesus as a prophet or teacher and as the living embodiment of God's word and presence. This revelation has deep implications for our faith and identity, as it ties us directly to the divine narrative that spans from the creation of the world to the life of Christ and beyond.

The Fall of the First Temple of God!

In Genesis 2:7, we find the account of God creating man from the dust of the ground, breathing into him the breath of life, thereby transforming him into a living being. This act of creation is deeply symbolic, illustrating both our humble origins and the divine spark that animates our existence. It signifies that while our physical bodies are of the earth, our true essence – our life force – is a gift from God.

Further along in Genesis 2:22-23, the narrative unfolds with the creation of Eve. God takes a rib from Adam and forms Eve, bringing her to Adam. This moment is significant, not only in terms of the creation of women but also in the establishment of human relationships. Adam's declaration, "This is now bone of my bones and flesh of my flesh; she shall be called Woman because she was taken out of Man," signifies the deep connection and unity between man and woman. It reflects a divine intention for companionship, partnership, and unity in the human experience.

This account provides more than just the origin of humanity; it offers insight into our interconnectedness and interdependence. The creation of Eve from Adam's rib symbolizes a shared essence, an inherent bond that goes beyond physicality. It speaks to the heart of human relationships – a connection that is not just physical but spiritual and emotional.

Focusing on the creation of Eve from Adam's rib, we find a powerful metaphor for the way God designs relationships and communities. It suggests that just as Eve was part of Adam, we are all intrinsically connected to one another. This connection is part of God's grand design, a reflection of His own relational nature as seen in the Trinity.

Understanding this aspect of our creation story enriches our perspective on human nature and purpose. It reminds us that we are not isolated beings but part of a larger, divinely orchestrated community. Our existence is not solitary; it is inherently linked to others, just as Eve was to Adam. This interconnectedness is a fundamental aspect of our identity, shaping how we live, relate, and find meaning in our lives.

As we conclude this chapter, we are called to reflect on the truths revealed in these early passages of Genesis. From the dust of the ground to the breath of life, from the formation of Adam to the creation of Eve, each element of these narratives speaks to the complexity and intentionality of God's design for humanity.

In the act of creation, we see a reflection of God's own nature – a God who is relational, loving, thoughtful, and purposeful. The creation of man and woman, from the same substance yet distinct, teaches us about the beauty of unity and diversity within God's plan. It reminds us that we are not random accidents of nature but carefully crafted beings imbued with the breath of the divine.

This understanding calls us to view our lives and relationships through a lens of sacredness and purpose. We are reminded that our existence is not a solitary journey but a shared experience enriched by our connections with others. Just as Eve was formed from Adam, we too are formed and influenced by our relationships with those around us, each interaction shaping our being in weighty ways.

In the creation of humanity, God laid the foundation for a story of love, relationship, and community. It is a story that finds its fullest expression in Jesus Christ, who came to restore and fulfill the divine plan disrupted by sin.

In Christ, we find not only a savior but also the perfect example of what it means to live in harmony with God and each other.

Chapter 2: Mary, God's Holy Temple

And God said, "Let there be a vault between the waters to separate water from water." So God made the vault and separated the water under the vault from the water above it. And it was so. God called the vault "sky." And there was evening, and there was morning—the second day.

And God said, "Let the water under the sky be gathered to one place, and let dry ground appear." And it was so. God called the dry ground "land," and the gathered waters he called "seas." And God saw that it was good.

-Genesis 1:5-10

Our expedition into the Holy Scriptures takes us deep into the book of Genesis as we begin to unravel its unfathomable mysteries. Much more than a record of past events, this sacred book contains a treasure trove of heavenly knowledge and prophetic symbolism. It establishes the groundwork for the millennial kingdom, which is not based on Earth but will be born out of the cosmic orchestration of destiny.

The poetic grandeur and narrative complexity of Genesis provide a backdrop for the earliest depictions of interactions between God and humans. Verse after verse, we see God's magnificent design come to fruition, from the creation of the world to the complex conversations between God and His creation, Adam and Eve. The first words that would resound through the ages, their complete meaning concealed until the end of time, were said here in the lush Eden, and they dealt with heavenly purpose and human destiny.

The deep significance of God's statements to Adam and Eve in these first chapters goes well beyond their original setting. These words may seem like plain old cautions or directions at first look, but upon deeper reflection, their prophetic character becomes clear, and they portend a new age. These verses attest to God's immutability and His sovereign purpose for the salvation of humanity; they are more than just artifacts from the past.

The more we examine these holy words, the more we see a pattern—a thread that is both subtle and obvious that runs through the story. Up until the proclamation of Jesus Christ's birth, this thread represented the hope of restoration, a reconstruction whose full significance would remain hidden. It was more than just an event in history. This revelation changed the trajectory of human history for all time. It was the fulfillment of a promise given from the beginning of time.

Jesus' miraculous birth fulfills the prophecies of these early debates about the restoration of God's kingdom. A new beginning, a divine intervention in the natural order of things, is symbolized by the seed of life, which is planted not in the rich soil of earth but in the pure, willing womb of Mary. As she humbly accepts this heavenly mission, Mary becomes more than the mother of the Savior—she becomes the alive and holy temple, the foundation upon which the New King will build His everlasting kingdom.

Faith and obedience are personified in Mary. Her earthly flesh becomes the conduit for the divine, the point where heaven and earth converge. The complexity and breadth of God's design for humanity are revealed to us by this great mystery, which illuminates our comprehension of His methods. The spiritual revelation that gives us a look into the very heart of God is the birth of Jesus, who was born of the Virgin Mary. It is more than just a historical event.

The famed "Catholic Saying" captures the core of Mary's participation in God's plan: SHE DID WHAT WE WILL LATER DO. We are all called to follow in Mary's footsteps and say "yes" to God, just as she did. A picture of genuine discipleship, her submission to God's will allowed for the greatest act of heavenly love—the birth of Jesus Christ—while her acceptance was more than just acquiescence.

In thinking about the birth of Jesus and Mary, we are enticed into the mystery of being "born again." This idea, which is fundamental to Christian theology, has its origins in the annunciation and the birth of Christ. Jesus' miraculous birth and Mary's submission to God's will provide us with a new perspective on rebirth as a spiritual awakening calling us to share in God's divine essence and transform into Christlikeness.

Let us, as we consider these facts, be receptive to the deep meaning of this divine story. Let us reflect on the vastness of God's love and the scope of His plan, which is laid out in Genesis and brought to fruition in the person of Jesus Christ, who was born of the Virgin Mary. As we travel this path, we are encouraged to take part in the divine drama of redemption, which has unfolded and will continue to unfold in the lives of believers throughout history.

The Virginal Birth as Rebuilding

Jesus birth through the Virgin Mary is a defining point in the history of God, illuminating his redemptive plan for mankind and placing us at the center of the divine narrative. This wondrous occurrence is pivotal in reestablishing harmony in the universe and ushering in a brand-new creation, and its theological importance is immense. The restoration of the personal relationship between God and His creation is marked by this occurrence, which is deep in its simplicity and grand in its ramifications. It represents the beginning of reconstructing what was lost.

Crucial to Christianity is the idea of the virgin birth, which defies rational explanation. This occurrence is a perfect illustration of how the supernatural meets the every day since it goes against the rules of nature. A new narrative of redemption and hope is being woven into the tapestry of human history by God's intervention in this remarkable event. This is more than just a random supernatural event; it is God's planned and orchestrated way of ushering in his New Kingdom, which will be marked by mercy, righteousness, and love from on high.

Symbolically and physically, Mary embodies a twofold function in her role as Jesus' mother. She physically represents the entrance of the Redeemer into human history. Where humanity and divinity meet, in the hallowed realm of her womb, the Word takes flesh and lives among us. This bodily part of Mary's role is central because it connects the heavenly story to the commonality of human experience. It is a concrete reminder that the plan of salvation from God is not some faraway idea but rather a real person who came to earth as a baby born into a lowly manger.

The new foundation that will be laid by the Kingdom of God is symbolized by Mary's womb. Like the soil, Mary takes in the divine promise and tends to it, just as a seed takes root in the soil. This act of cooperation between the divine and humans shows a lovely example of how God's kingdom is created, not by strength and dominion, but by humility, trust, and obedience. The way Mary willingly accepted her position exemplifies the answer God seeks from each of us: a heart that is receptive to His call and can nurture the growth of the divine seed.

Thus, the virginal birth exemplifies God's ability to produce life where there was none before, to make the impossible possible. It calls our assumptions about the universe into question and encourages us to accept a God-centered worldview that recognizes the supernatural. The New Kingdom, characterized by a suspension of the old norms and the establishment of a new order based on grace, love, and truth, is embodied in this remarkable occurrence.

Let the gravity of this event sink in as we reflect on the virginal birth and its significance. Praise be to God, whose love is so great that it came to earth in the most humane way possible—as a baby born to a virgin. This is the greatest mystery we will ever face. This deed shows us the plan for the New Kingdom, which will be established not by human might but by the humility and love of God.

The Part Mary Plays in God's Kingdom

As we ponder Mary's place in God's kingdom, we enter holy territory, investigating the delicate balancing act between her human nature and her heavenly calling. The life of Mary is a model of extreme modesty and grace. It tells the story of how God's salvation plan was set in motion by the faith of one woman and asks us to comprehend the human and divine aspects of that plan, living in perfect harmony with one another.

Mary's place in God's kingdom is based on her humanity. She was human, just like the rest of us—a young lady with aspirations, anxieties, and hopes. But she was also human, which gave her an extraordinary quality: a heart completely receptive to what God wanted. This extraordinary woman's response to Gabriel, "Behold, I am the servant of the Lord; let it be to me according to your word," reveals an uncommon and deep level of faithfulness and submission. Mary exemplifies the perfect human response to a divine calling: trusting in God's plan and humbly accepting it.

Though Mary's personal reaction is important, her duty goes beyond that. The redemption of humanity is set in motion when Mary reverses Eve's disobedience via her obedience. She was prepared to bear the Christ child, representing how open people are to receiving and caring for the holy spirit. Thus, the hallowed place where the seed of God's redeeming plan is planted and nurtured becomes the ground for the New King in Mary's womb.

There are many spiritual and theological meanings in the symbolism of Mary as the foundation for the King in his kingdom. When it comes to farming, the earth is like a nursery: it's the place where seeds are planted, and they take root and eventually flourish. This idea is personified by Mary, who is the mother of Jesus. She is like a garden where the heavenly Word grows lush and verdant. She nourished Jesus while he was still in his mother's womb, which is a picture of how believers should treat the Word. Believers are commanded to hold the Word in their hearts, letting it take root and change their lives, just as Mary held Jesus in her body.

Also, Mary is in a special position in God's kingdom because she is the mother of Jesus. She serves as an example of a disciple as well as a disciple herself. Her life is a perfect example of the faith, obedience, and love that define a relationship with God. From the Annunciation all the way to the Cross and beyond, Mary's journey exemplifies the profound faith and unyielding dedication to God's plan. Standing at the foot of the cross, she is a living testimony to her unfaltering faith; she is with Jesus throughout His ministry, seeing His miracles and hearing His teachings.

We are called to reflect on how we have responded to God's call on our life by looking at Mary's journey. We are encouraged to contemplate our personal spiritual journey as we continue to explore Mary's role in God's kingdom. Would we be prepared to lay down our lives for the coming king, just as Mary did? Can we let the holy seed that is inside us flourish and produce fruit? Following Mary's lead encourages us to accept our place in God's kingdom and take part in the heavenly story as it plays out in the world.

Mary unites humans with the divine and serves as a constant reminder that God's kingdom is not some faraway thing but something happening in our lives right now. She played an active part in God's kingdom, which is more than a historical truth; it has an effect on the spirituality and faith of people all across the globe.

The Incarnation and Divine Revelation

An unparalleled manifestation of the divine's hand in human history occurred during the birth of Jesus Christ, a moment that will go down in history as a watershed moment. The incarnation is more than the physical birth of a human being; it is the divine revelation of God's essence and relationship with humanity revealed via the incarnation of God into human flesh.

There is no way for humans to fully comprehend the Incarnation because it is a mystery. Jesus is the embodiment of God's decision to become entirely human while retaining his divine nature. This loving and modest deed reveals much about God's character. As a result, we see a God who is not cold and uncaring toward His creation but who becomes one of us and shares in our highs and lows. The incarnation of Jesus Christ reveals a God who is human like us, with all of our frailties and sufferings.

Also revealed in Jesus' birth is God's plan for the redemption of humanity. Christ has given us the means to go back on track with God by bridging the gap that sin created. Because of the incarnation, we see that God was prepared to do whatever it took to make up for what was lost when the Fall occurred. It is a heavenly intervention that initiates the New Kingdom and the redemption of the world.

A deeper understanding of God's nature is revealed through the Incarnation. The fact that God opted for Jesus to be born as a helpless baby demonstrates that He favors the poor and humble. The fact that Jesus was born in a lowly manger, far from the ostentation and splendor of worldly authority, demonstrates that God is one with the oppressed and the rejected. An impassioned plea for us to follow God's example of humility and care for the least of us makes a strong statement about God's priorities.

Looking into the Catholic proverb about Mary's "yes" to God reveals another dimension of the Incarnation. "Let it be to me according to your word," Mary told Gabriel, transcending the mere reception of a message from on high.

In response to God's initiative, it exemplifies the perfect human reaction. Despite the danger and uncertainty, Mary said "yes" because she trusted God's plan and was eager to be used by God. Her answer exemplifies genuine trust, which is not conditional on miraculous events but based on God's word's promise.

The cooperative nature of God's operation in the world is further emphasized by this phrase. Despite God's omnipotence and ability to fulfill His objectives alone, He prefers to do it via willing individuals like Mary. This human-heavenly partnership exemplifies a fundamental feature of God's kingdom. That kingdom is based on faith and obedience, and it is a place where God's people work together to do His will.

The examination of Mary's "yes" also prompts us to reflect on how we have responded to God's invitation. Following in Mary's footsteps, who was instrumental in the Incarnation, God invites us to join him in his continuing mission in the world. Even if the world's Savior doesn't come into being because of our "yes," it can change lives and make God more present wherever we go.

The Incarnation and Mary's reaction deepen our comprehension of God's love and our place in His holy scheme. A vivid reminder of how divine grace and human cooperation can work together to bring about God's objectives is the birth of Jesus and Mary's 'yes' to God.

Being Born Again: A New Understanding

Finally, as we near the end of this chapter, we reach a crucial and life-altering idea in Christian belief: being "born again." This idea has a deep spiritual meaning, has a special relationship to Mary and the birth of Jesus, and provides a fresh perspective on our own spiritual rebirth and its ramifications.

The account of Mary's life and the birth of Jesus offers a potent allegory for the rebirth process. We are likewise commanded to receive the Word of God in our hearts and let it change us from the inside out, just as Mary did when she carried Jesus into the world. A significant inner shift happens when we allow the transforming power of God's grace to take place in us; this is not the same as a physical rebirth. A new awareness of who we are and what we're here to do as God's children characterizes this spiritually born second birth rather than a physical one.

The connection between Mary's birth and the rebirth sheds light on the importance of trust and submission in our spiritual development. A new life in Christ necessitates a heart position akin to Mary's "yes" to God, which was an act of obedience and faith. It calls us to put our faith in Christ and our old selves aside. Instead of being a one-and-done deal, this is an ongoing process of maturation and change through which we are molded into more like Christ.

Being born again has extensive and deep-seated consequences. It marks a transition from a distant to an intimate connection with God. Our perspective on life, our relationships, and everything in them shifts as a result. A new sense of purpose, direction, and meaning is bestowed upon us when we are born again, and that direction is to serve, love, and obey God.

The new community known as the body of Christ is another gift of this rebirth. We are invited to support, encourage, and grow in faith together as a community, just as Mary was not alone on her journey. Being born again has a communal component that calls us to act out our faith in community rather than in isolation.

In addition, the act of being born again opens the door for us to take part in the unfolding narrative of God's salvific action on earth. We are not on the sidelines but rather called to be witnesses for Christ and to share the good news of Jesus Christ with the world. Through the work of the Holy Spirit, we are changed and able to bear witness to God's grace and love.

Ultimately, the idea of being reborn is woven into a rich fabric of spiritual and theological truths through its connections to the birth of Jesus and Mary. A connection with God characterized by trust, submission, and change is what it beckons us toward. As we ponder this deep reality, let us welcome the path of rebirth and let it influence all parts of our lives. Doing so enables us to fully embrace our identity as God's children, experiencing firsthand the New Kingdom that was ushered in by Jesus' birth and modeled by Mary's steadfast trust and obedience.

Chapter 3: The Delivery of the Promise of God

"And God said, "Let there be lights in the vault of the sky to separate the day from the night, and let them serve as signs to mark sacred times, and days and years, and let them be lights in the vault of the sky to give light on the earth." And it was so. God made two great lights—the greater light to govern the day and the lesser light to govern the night. He also made the stars. God set them in the vault of the sky to give light on the earth, to govern the day and the night, and to separate light from darkness. And God saw that it was good. And there was evening, and there was morning—the fourth day."

-Genesis 1:14-19

God spoke creation into existence with His Word. That is all it took for him—just one word from the utterance of which light separated the darkness in a literal sense. It was as if everything fell into place when that one word was uttered. Everything then made sense.

In the same way, He agreed that the universe should have Jesus. With His approval, just like that, the arrival of Jesus marked a new era entirely.

Incarnation as the Fulfillment of the Promise

In the Bible's narrative, the incarnation of Jesus Christ stands as a monumental fulfillment of God's longstanding promises. This important event showed what the New Kingdom would be like and served as a deep fulfillment of prophecy. The Word took on human form and divine essence to live among us and lead us to spiritual renewal and life in the kingdom.

The promise of a Savior has been a part of biblical history since the first prophecies in the Old Testament. The prophets talked about a Messiah who would save people—a servant who would die for many people's sins.

As an example, Isaiah spoke about the birth of a unique child who would carry a kingdom and be known as the Wonderful Counselor, the Mighty God, the Everlasting Father, and the Prince of Peace (Isaiah 9:6). This prophecy, which talks about divine rule and endless peace, shows that the promised Messiah will be both God and a person.

The fact that these predictions came true in Jesus is not just a fact; it is a spiritual reality that changes lives. The world got its first look at God's kingdom coming to life through the life of a single person when Jesus was born in a stable.

The most important parts of these ancient predictions are His lessons, miracles, and, finally, His death as a sacrifice and resurrection. Each step of His trip on earth was a sign of divine truth that showed God's plan to save people and fix the broken relationship between God and people.

When we look at a broader perspective, imagine a God so vast and powerful that creating the universe was just a word. Even though he has done all those powerful things, he still chooses to become a tiny, fragile baby. That is indeed the mind-blowing truth of Jesus—fully God yet fully human. He wasn't just some powerful being looking down on us. He felt hunger pangs, the sting of sadness, and the crushing weight of pain, just like us.

This might seem confusing, but it's the very reason Jesus is our bridge to God. He understands our struggles because he walked the same path, facing every temptation we do without succumbing to sin (Hebrews 4:15). He's not some distant figure judging us, but someone who truly gets it.

Knowing Jesus was born as a human fills our hearts with hope. It whispers, "God cares deeply. He's not some unfeeling force but intricately woven into the fabric of our lives." It all makes sense because he was one of us. This is why it is easier for us to talk to him with open hearts, knowing he understands our weaknesses and burdens.

The Incarnation—Jesus becoming flesh—is a love story for the ages. It's a love that shattered the boundaries between heaven and earth, a love so immense that it conquered the chasm of sin and separation. God, out of his overflowing love, stepped into our messy world and sacrificed his power to pull us back into the light of his grace and truth.

This isn't just theology; it's a life-changing truth. It strengthens our faith, deepens our understanding, and ignites a fire within us. We feel compelled to live a life that reflects this closeness to Jesus and to share this incredible love with a world desperately needing it.

Seeing the Incarnation as the fulfillment of God's promises fills us with renewed devotion and an electrifying sense of purpose. We become determined to carry on Jesus' mission, building his kingdom here on earth, one act of love at a time.

The New Kingdom Revealed Through Jesus

The revelation of the New Kingdom via Jesus Christ was not just about the arrival of a Savior; it was also about uncovering a way of living that would completely transform one's existence. Jesus provided a vivid image of what the Kingdom of God looks like via the teachings, parables, and miracles that He performed among his followers. The principles that define this kingdom were made abundantly evident to believers via his mission on earth, and these values continue to serve as a compass for believers even in the present day.

Jesus, that master storyteller, loved using parables to crack open spiritual truths. Remember the tiny mustard seed that sprouted into a giant tree, a haven for birds? What if that story held a secret about God's kingdom?

Could it be that something as small and ordinary as a mustard seed represents the humble beginnings of this kingdom? A kingdom destined to soar, offering shelter and meaning to a vast multitude, just like the birds nestled in the tree's branches?

This parable begs a question: isn't it fascinating how greatness can blossom from seemingly insignificant seeds? Maybe those small steps of faith we take, the ones that feel inconsequential, hold the potential for incredible impact. It makes you wonder, doesn't it? What seeds of faith are we planting today that might one day become towering testaments to God's work in the world?

One more compelling illustration of the principles of the kingdom can be seen in the miracles that Jesus performed.

Here, Jesus was doing more than just providing a supper when He fed the five thousand with only five loaves of bread and two fish; He was displaying God's provision and the fullness that is found in the Kingdom of God. In the Kingdom of God, there is provision for all individuals, and the charity of God is beyond the limit, as demonstrated by this miraculous occurrence. Believers in the modern day are challenged to put their faith in God's provision and to demonstrate generosity in their own lives through this passage.

In a world where the outcasts, the broken, the ones society pushes to the fringes, are embraced with open arms, is the world worth living in? This was the radical message Jesus preached through his very relationships. He saw past the labels—the sick, the poor, the sinners—and saw people worthy of love. He healed the ostracized and shared meals with the condemned, shattering the barriers that kept people from God.

This wasn't just a social revolution; it was a glimpse into the heart of God's kingdom. A kingdom where everyone, regardless of their past or imperfections, has a place. It challenges us to look beyond the surface and see the humanity in everyone we meet. It compels us to offer grace and love freely, just as Jesus did.

But Jesus didn't stop there. He raised the bar even higher, calling for compassion not just for the forgotten but even for our enemies. He taught us to love one another with the same fierce, unconditional love he had for us. It's a call that tugs at our hearts, urging us to move beyond self-interest and embrace a life of service. A life where the joy of others becomes a reflection of our own spiritual growth.

This isn't about following a set of rules; it's about aligning ourselves with the love Jesus embodied. It's a call to humility, a call to see ourselves as servants, just as he served. It's a call to build a community where love, not judgment, reigns supreme. It's a call that stirs something deep within us, a call to be the reflection of God's boundless love in a world that desperately needs it.

Jesus' actions and teachings weren't meant to be museum pieces admired from afar. So, for believers today, the question becomes: how do we get involved? How can we take these amazing ideals of the kingdom—humility, justice, and kindness—and make them real in our own lives?

How would it feel to be in a world where despair gives way to hope and violence surrenders to peace? That's the promise of the kingdom, but it won't happen by itself. Could we be the ones to bring that light into the darkness?

Maybe it's not about grand gestures but about the choices we make every day. Can we be a source of strength for someone struggling? Can we stand up for what's right, even when it's difficult? Can we show kindness, even to those who don't deserve it?

These are the questions that can ignite a fire within us. Because isn't that the ultimate goal? To be living testaments to God's kingdom here on earth? The answer lies not just in our hearts but in the actions we take. What will our contribution be? How will we help build the kingdom, one act of love at a time?

Transformation into the Temple of God

The New Testament showcases the idea that Christians are under transformation into the Temple of God., which is a huge change in how people think about God's presence among His people. This change affects the individuals and the faith group as a whole, affecting how they live their daily lives and communicate with each other.

When writing to Christians, the Apostle Paul stresses over and over that those who believe are not only followers of Christ but also the very place where God's Spirit lives. "Don't you know that you are God's house and that the Holy Spirit lives in you?" (1 Cor. 3:16).

People who believe in God are challenged by this question to see how sacred their bodies are and the huge duty that comes with being alive. It means a call to be pure and honest and follow the Spirit's guidance in life, staying away from actions that would dishonor this holy place.

What if our bodies were not made from flesh and bone and were sacred vessels? It would be a temple, no less, one that was chosen to house the very presence of God. What would that change?

In actuality, everything. Suddenly, self-care wouldn't be a chore but an act of worship. You'd nourish your body with respect, banish harmful habits, and guard your thoughts with the same reverence you'd show a holy sanctuary. Holiness wouldn't be a burden but a beautiful reflection of the divine residing within. Every word and every choice would vibrate with the awareness that you carry a spark of God's light.

You have to know that this transformation here isn't just about you. Wouldn't our churches crackle with a new kind of energy? Unity wouldn't be a lofty ideal, but it is the natural consequence of hearts all attuned to the same divine presence. Respect and love would flow effortlessly as we recognize the temple of God, not just in ourselves but in every brother and sister in Christ. We wouldn't be bricks in a building but living stones, forming a magnificent spiritual edifice together, just as Peter described (1 Peter 2:5).

Think about it. Wouldn't this shatter the limitations of physical structures? Suddenly, the church wouldn't be confined to walls. We could gather in homes, parks, or even virtually, and the sacredness wouldn't diminish because the truest church isn't a place but a collective of hearts where God resides. This flexibility becomes a lifeline in times of hardship when traditional worship seems out of reach. The divine light can still shine, carried by a community of walking temples.

And this light wouldn't stay contained. We, as vessels of God's love, would be compelled to carry it outward. Imagine workplaces, schools, and neighborhoods transformed by the kindness, justice, and mercy radiating from within us. Every act of compassion would be a beacon, drawing others closer to the love that resides within each of us. Wouldn't that be a world worth living in? A world where every person becomes a temple, and together, we build a society bathed in the light of God's presence?

Becoming a dwelling place for the Holy Spirit is not a goal in and of itself but rather a channel through which the redeeming purpose of God can be made apparent. After receiving Christ's sanctifying grace and the Holy Spirit's indwelling, every believer plays an essential role in the unfolding drama of God's kingdom on earth and is given the means to continue Christ's mission. Therefore, being a house of worship for God is a constant call to holiness, a means of strengthening relationships with others, and a part of God's redemptive plan for the world.

The Role of Believers as Building Blocks in the Spiritual Kingdom

Have you ever stopped to consider the sheer audacity of God's plan? This grand, sprawling kingdom is not built with mortar and stone but with living, breathing people! Each believer—you, me, everyone—are we bricks? Sure, that's the basic idea, but is that all there is to it?

If you think of a builder who is not your average Joe with a trowel but a cosmic architect wielding the very fabric of existence, He doesn't just toss together a wobbly wall with mismatched bricks. This is a masterpiece in the making! Each brick, each believer, is meticulously chosen, honed by the Word of God, and ignited by the Holy Spirit. We're not just filler blocks; we're the stained glass, the support beams, and the very foundation stones!

Think about it! Each and every one of us is crucial to the church's strength and resilience. On the other hand, imagine the beauty that would emerge from a structure where every brick is precisely laid and exudes conviction and direction. A star that shines brightly enough to be seen from space—a monument to the might of the church when its members work together?

This isn't merely a wall of metaphor. What we have here is considerably more amazing; it is the body of Christ, a live, breathing entity! Inside this body, every believer is vital.

This interconnectedness within the body of Christ means that every believer has a unique contribution that only they can provide. Whether it's through teaching, encouragement, serving, or leading, each action adds to the church's overall mission.

The Apostle Paul speaks of the church as a body with many parts, each with a different function. In his letters, he emphasizes that no part is dispensable or less important than another. This analogy is powerful—it tells us that the diversity of gifts and callings within the church is not only natural but necessary for the body to function optimally. Just as eyes, hands, and feet contribute differently to a person's daily activities, so too do various believers contribute differently to the church's life.

This diversity within unity has practical implications for how believers live out their faith in the community. Being humble and realizing that everyone has something useful to give is what it calls for. It requires working together since reaching shared goals takes a lot of time. It also encourages love and respect for each other, knowing that each person, no matter what part they play, is important for the church's mission and well-being.

The spiritual structure of God's kingdom is strengthened by Christians fulfilling these roles. They don't just sit on their faith; it becomes active. Doing things out of faith, like helping those in need, teaching God's Word, spreading the gospel, and comforting the sad, doesn't just fulfill one's religious duties; it makes the whole society stronger. These are the ways that God's love and forgiveness show up in the world.

The role of believers as building blocks in God's kingdom also extends beyond the confines of church activities. Each believer carries the presence of God into their daily environments—homes, workplaces, schools, and beyond. Living out the values taught by Jesus, believers influence these spheres, which is the way to bring the principles of the Kingdom into everyday life. This influence is subtle yet profound, as it can transform societies by introducing godly values into secular spaces.

As believers live the Word, their lives demonstrate God's transformation. They are active participants in a divine mission, establishing the kingdom with each faith-filled activity. In their many duties and efforts, believers build a spiritual building that withstands time and shows God's grace and truth to the world.

Divine Union:

"I am in my Father, and you are in me, and I am in you." Content Focus: "In that day, you will know that I am in my Father, and you are in me, and I am in you."

In the Christian faith, few scriptures entirely capture the intimacy and mystery of our relationship with Christ as poignantly as John 14:20: "In that day, you will know that I am in my Father, and you are in me, and I am in you." This promise from Jesus to His disciples isn't just a statement; it's an invitation into the divine dance of unity and love.

This divine union between Christ and Christians is not just an idea to be studied; it's an experience that changes who we are, what we're here to do, and how we live our lives. This deep spiritual link can change how we see ourselves and how we deal with the world around us if we understand and accept it.

Now, for a moment, erase everything from your mind and try to understand the emotional depth and security that come from knowing that Christ Himself is in us and we are in Him. This knowledge brings an overwhelming sense of belonging and acceptance that can soothe the most troubled heart. It tells us that we are not just wandering through life alone but are intimately connected with Christ and, through Him, to the very heart of God.

When Jesus declares that He is in the Father, and we are in Him, and He is in us, He is speaking of a unity that transcends physical presence—it's a spiritual and eternal connection that assures us of His continual presence and work in our lives. This union means that in every challenge, every joy, every trial, and every victory, Christ is with us, experiencing it with us and guiding us through it.

The implications of this truth are vast for our daily lives. When you know that Christ dwells within you, your approach to life changes. You are driven by a love that is not your own; you forgive more easily; you seek to serve rather than be served; and you express joy in situations where it seems impossible. This is not because of some human effort but because the life of Christ is being manifested in your actions and attitudes.

When you enter communal worship, you're not just singing hymns or listening to a sermon. You're stepping into a shared experience—a heart-thumping, soul-stirring encounter with

God's presence. It's not a distant echo but a tangible electricity that crackles between you, the person next to you, and the one across the room.

Why? Because in that moment, you realize something profound. Christ isn't just some faraway deity, a figure in a stained-glass window. He's here, right here, burning brightly within each and every one of you. Doesn't that send shivers down your spine? Suddenly, the feeling of community explodes. You're not just strangers sitting in pews; you're a tapestry woven together by the very thread of Christ's love.

And this connection isn't just about warm fuzzies. It ignites a fire within you. Knowing Jesus lives in you and that you're an extension of his love doesn't that fill you with an intoxicating courage? The courage to step outside your comfort zone, to speak words of hope that mend broken hearts, and to reach out with compassion that transforms lives. You become His hands and feet, not because you're some superhero, but because His power surges through you, empowering you to be a beacon of light in a world that desperately needs it.

The next time you raise your voice in worship, don't just go through the motions. Feel it. Feel the connection, the shared presence, and the power that courses through this community of believers. Because in that moment, something extraordinary happens. You become more than yourself; you become a living testament to the transformative power of Christ's love. Isn't that a truth worth celebrating?

Let the reality of Christ in us inspire us to live boldly and lovingly. Let it challenge us to look beyond our limitations and see the possibilities of what God can do through us. Let it remind us that in every moment of every day, we are never alone, for Christ is in us, and we are in Him, and through this divine union, we are connected to the infinite love and power of God Himself.

Chapter 4: Tearing Down of The Old and Building The New

"And God said, 'Let the water under the sky be gathered to one place, and let dry ground appear.' And it was so. God called the dry ground 'land,' and the gathered waters he called 'seas.' And God saw that it was good. Then God said, 'Let the land produce vegetation: seed-bearing plants and trees on the land that bear fruit with seed in it, according to their various kinds.' And it was so."

-Genesis 1:9-11

God's intentions for creation are clearly mentioned in the scriptures. He laid the foundations of creation with purpose and intention. It was He who spoke life into being and shaped the natural world into a harmonious ecosystem.

However, the creation seemed to be different when Jesus and His disciples looked upon the magnificent Jewish temple. It was no more than a marvel of human craftsmanship. The temple stood as a symbol of religious devotion, cultural identity, and national pride.

Shocking? Not at all. The believers know it was foretold. Jesus had blessed us with the knowledge already in His declaration. *"Do you see all these things? Truly I tell you, not one stone here will be left on another; everyone will be thrown down."* - Matthew 24:2.

To understand the shock of this prophecy, we must grasp the historical and religious significance of the temple to the Jewish people. The temple was more than just an architectural wonder; it was the spiritual center of Jewish worship. It was built on Mount Moriah, where Abraham once offered Isaac. If we look at its origin, it was initially constructed by King Solomon. At that time, the temple was a place where heaven and earth intersected. The inner sanctuary, the Holy of Holies, was considered God's earthly dwelling place. Every year, millions of Jews journeyed to Jerusalem to offer sacrifices and celebrate the holy festivals.

After Solomon's temple was destroyed by the Babylonians, the Jews rebuilt it, and Herod the Great later expanded and adorned it with marble, gold, and precious stones.

When the time of Jesus came, in that period, the temple was the crowning jewel of Jerusalem—a symbol of Israel's resilience and divine favor. The disciples marveled at its grandeur. They pointed out its impressive stones and beautiful architecture and glorified its beauty. For Jesus, it was nothing but a structure of stone. He saw beyond the glittering facade and spoke of its impending ruin.

Jesus' prediction of the temple's destruction must have been startling, even unsettling, to His disciples. For centuries, the temple had stood as a testament to God's covenant with Israel. *How can it mean nothing?* Its destruction implied a seismic shift in religious understanding and practice. In fact, Jesus' prophecy was fulfilled in AD 70 when the Romans destroyed Jerusalem and the temple. The sacred structure was reduced to rubble, leaving not one stone on another.

The prophecy mentioned above was a precursor to the creation of a novel spiritual sanctuary. This sanctuary was not constructed by human hands but rather erected on the basis of Jesus Christ Himself, serving as its foundation. Apostle Paul captures this vision in Ephesians 2:19-22, writing, *"Consequently, you are no longer foreigners and strangers, but fellow citizens with God's people and also members of His household, built on the foundation of the apostles and prophets, with Christ Jesus Himself as the chief cornerstone. In Him, the whole building is joined together and rises to become a holy temple in the Lord. And in Him, you too are being built together to become a dwelling in which God lives by His Spirit."*

Jesus' prophecy about the destruction of the man-made temple reveals God's plan to replace the old system of worship with a new covenant community. This new community was the Church. They would not be bound to a single geographic location but would become a living temple spread across the world, composed of people from every nation and tribe.

Just as God gathered the waters together and brought forth dry land in Genesis, He gathered believers together and brought forth a new spiritual creation—a temple built on the cornerstone of Jesus Christ. The tearing down of the old was necessary to build the new. For God was establishing a Kingdom not made of stone but one comprised of gold. One that had the power to transform the hearts and lives by His Word and Spirit.

The Old Temple vs. The New Spiritual Temple

For centuries, the Jewish temple stood at the heart of religious life in Jerusalem. Its imposing architecture and elaborate rituals were not merely for show. They signified the temple's role as a place where God met His people, and His people offered sacrifices and prayers in return. It was a sacred space that held the essence of Jewish identity and faith. Here, pilgrims would journey from distant lands to present their offerings and celebrate Passover, Yom Kippur, and other festivals. The temple was more than a building; it was a symbol of God's stable presence and favor.

Like always, Jesus had predicted a dramatic change that would come forth in his people. He said in Matthew 24:2, *"Do you see all these things? Truly, I tell you, not one stone here will be left on another; everyone will be thrown down."* This prediction was fulfilled in AD 70 when the Roman army destroyed the temple. The ruins symbolized the end of the old system of worship and the beginning of a new covenant.

In the new covenant, Jesus himself is the cornerstone of a new spiritual temple. This temple is not defined by walls or geography, but it is made up of believers. Paul tells us in Ephesians 2:19-22 that through Christ, Jews and Gentiles alike are joined together as members of God's household and form a holy temple in the Lord. Jesus' prophecy of the physical temple's destruction symbolized a transformation in the way humanity relates to God. No longer would worship be tied to a specific place. Instead, it would transcend physical structures and geographic boundaries, focusing on spiritual principles rather than rituals.

To gather a clear idea in relation to the transformation, we have to consider the symbolism behind Jesus' words and actions. Jesus highlighted that the new spiritual temple would not rely on sacrifices or rituals by driving out the money changers from the temple and stating that His body is the new temple that would be demolished and rebuilt in three days. He did this by destroying the temple and beginning the rebuilding process. In its place, it would be characterized by trust and the presence of the Holy Spirit within one's being.

In practical terms, this new temple means that believers are the dwelling place of God. Wherever a believer goes, there is a holy space where God resides for them to look over to and worship. This has far-reaching implications for how Christians see themselves and how they relate to others. If you consider yourself a temple of the Holy Spirit, your everyday actions take on greater significance. How you treat others, work, and spend your time reflects your role as God's dwelling place.

Believers are not only individual temples but also interconnected parts of the broader body of Christ. Every soul is interconnected in practice and in calling out to the One who releases all the blessings. In this spiritual temple, each member has a role to play, and every contribution is valuable.

Suppose we take the example of people who are gifted in teaching while others may have positive traits in hospitality or administration. Humans have different traits. Just as the physical temple had various functions and rooms for different rituals. The new spiritual temple comprises diverse people with different gifts, all working together to fulfill God's purpose.

As believers, to truly understand this transformation and confirm that it aligns with the Jewish faith, we need to see what the outcome is. This is the fulfillment of God's promises eventually, and we see clear evidence. God intended that His people would be a light to all nations, and the new spiritual temple allowed this light to shine brightly. The rituals and sacrifices of the old temple pointed to a greater reality—a Messiah who would ultimately reconcile humanity to God.

Now, this reconciliation is available to everyone who believes in it, and it is manifested through a living, breathing temple that spans the globe.

The Transfiguration - A Glimpse of Future Glory

The Transfiguration of Jesus Christ is one of the most remarkable events in the Gospels. It's a moment when Jesus' divine nature is revealed to His closest disciples, Peter, James, and John. It gives them a foretaste of the glorified state that He—and eventually they—would possess in the coming Kingdom. This extraordinary experience is clearly recorded in Matthew 17, Mark 9, and Luke 9, and it provides a philosophical insight into the nature of Jesus' divinity and the transformation awaiting believers.

The Transfiguration begins when Jesus leads Peter, James, and John up a high mountain. There, His face shines like the sun, and His clothes become dazzling white. In this radiant transformative state, Jesus speaks with Moses and Elijah. Ther he represents the Law and the Prophets, respectively. The presence of Moses and Elijah underscores how Jesus' ministry fulfills the prophecies and legal requirements that came before.

They discussed the impending fulfillment of Jesus' mission in Jerusalem together, where He would suffer, die, and rise again.

This event signified more than just a glimpse into Jesus' divine glory; it symbolically ties His work to the history and purpose of God's covenant people. Moses and Elijah had both met with God on mountains in the Old Testament. Moses received the Law on Mount Sinai, and Elijah encountered God on Mount Horeb. Now, on this high mountain, Jesus stands in conversation with them, solidifying His role as the culmination of God's promises and the inauguration of a new covenant.

Peter had been overwhelmed by the radiant sight and, understood its gravity, suggested building three shelters: one each for Jesus, Moses, and Elijah. In his zeal, he desired to capture and preserve this divine encounter. While he still spoke, a bright cloud enveloped them, and the voice of God declared in Matthew 17:5, *"This is my Son, whom I love; with Him, I am well pleased. Listen to Him!"* This declaration reminded Peter and the other disciples that Jesus is the ultimate revelation of God's will.

Peter's reaction reflected human nature's impulse to hold onto spiritual highs and unforgettable moments of revelation. When we look at our own lives, we often want to linger in those instances where we sense God's presence most clearly. This often occurs during a powerful worship experience or after an answered prayer. However, Jesus doesn't intend for His disciples to remain on the mountain but calls them to return to the valleys below, where His ministry of healing, teaching, and redemption continues.

The Transfiguration reveals the ultimate glorified state that Jesus will assume after His resurrection, but it also provides a glimpse into the transformation awaiting all believers. The Apostle Paul reminds us that, through Christ, we will one day be transformed into glorious bodies like His, free from corruption and death (Philippians 3:21). The Transfiguration, therefore, serves as a hopeful vision of what awaits those who follow Jesus into His Kingdom.

In the future transformed Kingdom, there will be no pain, mourning, or death. God's people will be radiant with Christ's glory, living in perfect harmony with Him and each other. This future isn't just about individual glorification but also about community. Like Peter, James, and John on the mountain, we will stand in the company of the saints, enveloped by God's loving presence and fulfilling the promises of old.

It gives us a foretaste of this incredible future and urges us to listen to Jesus and remain faithful. It's true that our present sufferings cannot be compared to the glory that will be revealed. The radiance of Christ on that mountain reminds us that, through Him, we will shine with the brilliance of God's love and mercy, reflecting the divine image we were always meant to embody.

The Old Law Fulfilled and Transcended by Jesus

The relationship between Jesus and the Old Law is one of fulfillment and transcendence. When Jesus said, *"Do not think that I have come to abolish the Law or the Prophets; I have not come to abolish them but to fulfill them"* (Matthew 5:17), He wasn't dismissing centuries of Jewish tradition but was pointing to something greater—a new standard rooted in love and grace.

His teachings and ultimate sacrifice showed how the Old Testament laws, valuable as they were, were only shadows of the full reality that was revealed in Him.

To grasp this fulfillment, we must understand the purpose of the Old Law. It provided guidance on how to live, worship, and approach God. It also revealed the nature of sin and pointed forward to a Messiah who perfectly embodies the law's principles and provides the ultimate means of atonement. The Old Law served as a tutor, guiding people toward the truth that Jesus would later embody.

In practice, Jesus transcended the old law by shifting the focus from external compliance to internal transformation. In the Sermon on the Mount, He used phrases like, *"You have heard that it was said... But I tell you..." (Matthew* 5:21-22) to show that mere observance of rules wasn't enough; one must also address the heart's condition. Jesus' teachings went beyond the Old Law, which prohibited murder, by emphasizing that holding anger against someone could be equally harmful. As he focused on the underlying motives, He raised the standard to a level that surpassed mere compliance with outward rules, inspiring a heart that abounds with love.

In today's world, many laws and regulations govern our behavior, whether driving safely or paying taxes. It is Jesus' teaching that calls us to a higher standard than merely obeying the rules. For instance, paying taxes isn't just about fulfilling a legal obligation; it's also about being a good steward of public resources and supporting services that benefit society. Likewise, adhering to road safety isn't simply avoiding fines; it's about valuing the lives of those we share the road with.

Jesus' higher standard is most visible in His command to love our enemies and pray for those who persecute us (Matthew 5:44). This teaching was revolutionary because it required people to extend grace beyond their social circles. In practice, this means forgiving those who wrong us and showing compassion to people we may not naturally agree with or like.

Jesus' teachings on generosity provide an excellent example of how we can become more giving and empathetic towards others. One of the most notable instances is when he lauded the widow who offered her the last two coins, highlighting the importance of giving with a pure heart rather than being preoccupied with the amount. This principle continues to inspire us to give selflessly, acknowledging that everything we possess is a blessing from God and that we should respect and share our blessings with others.

Living by this new standard requires internalizing Jesus' teachings and surrendering to His transformative grace. Believers can embody this standard in their daily lives by reflecting on their motives. They need to be mindful of the way their actions impact others. The place and time don't matter, for the rules are universal and applicable at every second of our lives. Whether it's at work, at home, or in the community, believers should actively seek opportunities to practice kindness, patience, and humility.

Jesus didn't replace the Old Law with a new set of rules but ushered in a spirit-led ethic of love, mercy, and grace. This standard isn't achieved through strict adherence to rituals but through a heart attuned to God's will and a life yielded to His Spirit. If we follow His example as believers, we can go beyond mere religious practices and live out the radical, all-encompassing love that Jesus modeled. It is love that fulfills and goes beyond the letter of the law.

The New Covenant Community - A United Body of Believers

The establishment of the New Covenant community, the Church, signifies the birth of something extraordinary. Through this birth, we got to know that it is a united body of believers overcoming cultural and religious barriers. In all aspects of the life, death, and resurrection of Jesus, a new community was formed, no longer limited by ethnicity, language, or status but united in faith and purpose. This revolutionary unity makes the Church, unlike any other institution, reflect the principles of the New Kingdom and serve as a beacon of hope for a divided world.

The Church was born at Pentecost when the Holy Spirit descended upon the disciples. It empowered them to spread the message of Jesus to the nations. People from various regions, cultures, and languages heard the gospel in their own tongue and were drawn together by a shared belief in Christ.

This miraculous event laid the foundation for a community that would become known as the Body of Christ. As the Apostle Paul wrote in 1 Corinthians 12:12-13, *"Just as a body, though one, has many parts, but all its many parts form one body, so it is with Christ. For we were all baptized by one Spirit so as to form one body."*

In tangibility, it means that believers are not isolated individuals but interconnected parts of a greater whole. The diversity of the body is essential to its functioning. Some are called to teach, some to serve, some to lead, and others to encourage. The beauty of this diversity is evident in everyday life.

In a local church, you may find an engineer teaching Bible studies, a retiree organizing food drives, a nurse offering prayer and counsel, and a young parent leading worship.

A person's unique combination of experiences, viewpoints, and abilities makes them unique. Even though we're all unique, the Holy Spirit uses our unique qualities to unite us in Christ. This harmony does not stem from a need for everyone to act in the same way but from a common goal of improving society as a whole. It is possible to build a varied and peaceful community that accepts and celebrates each person for what they bring to the table.

But what does this unity truly mean in the face of a world marked by division?

Would a disagreement over politics, economic disparity, or cultural differences be considered a community problem?

Consider a community project where members of a church come together to help rebuild a home damaged by natural disasters. The volunteers, regardless of age, social or financial status, or ethnicity, work side by side, not because of any personal gain. It is their belief that makes them show love to those in need. This kind of unity, rooted in a shared faith, goes beyond superficial differences and reflects the selfless love that Jesus commanded.

The unity within the New Covenant community also reflects the principles of the New Kingdom. In the Church, distinctions that often separate people—like gender, ethnicity, or status—

lose their power. Paul emphasized in the following verse that highlighted the truth in Galatians 3:28: *"There is neither Jew nor Gentile, neither slave nor free, nor is there male and female, for you are all one in Christ Jesus."* This doesn't mean that differences cease to exist but that in Christ, they are celebrated as a reflection of God's creativity and are no longer a cause for division.

The New Covenant unites individuals to work towards a common mission. They are called upon to propagate God's Kingdom by nurturing disciples, extending care to the underprivileged, and exemplifying love and compassion in their interactions. When believers take up the responsibility of being ambassadors of reconciliation, the Church emerges as a formidable example for the world. This body ends up illustrating that true harmony is achievable through Christ.

Building Up the New Temple: The New Life in Christ

To live a life in Christ is a transformative experience for the body and the soul. It's more than a new beginning or a change of direction. It is what creates a resounding shift in the heart. Why? For it is an invitation to become part of something bigger than ourselves. Each one of us, as individuals, is called to live out a new identity in Christ. Together, we're building a spiritual temple, brick by brick, by living out the principles of the New Kingdom.

In his first letter, the Apostle Peter tells us we are *"living stones,"* being crafted into a spiritual house (1 Peter 2:5). We each have a role to play in this grand design, whether we're teachers, nurses, chefs, accountants, or homemakers. When you accepted Christ, that is when you were given a purpose that goes beyond the limits of earthly titles and achievements. You are not defined by your past mistakes, current struggles, or future fears. You are *whole* because of God's incredible grace.

As for the temple, one might ask, what does it mean to be a living stone, to be part of this temple?

It means living out Kingdom values like love, service, and humility. According to what Jesus demonstrated to us, love is limitless and unrestricted. It is about having a high level of compassion for other people and forgiving them deeply. Making an effort to help others by, for example, preparing a dinner for a neighbor who is going through a difficult time or volunteering to listen to a friend who is going through a difficult time. In addition, humility is the acknowledgment that every gift we possess is a gift from God. It is important to remember that God encourages us to use our gifts for the benefit of other people.

If you're an artist, maybe your gift could uplift others through worship. If you're a compassionate listener, perhaps you can offer solace to someone going through a rough time. Are you organized and detail-oriented? You could help with planning and logistics. When we offer our unique gifts, we strengthen the entire community of faith and enrich the spiritual temple.

If we look at a local church community that lives out these values daily, we see diversity. They welcome people of all backgrounds with open arms. They organize food drives for those in need, visit the sick, and volunteer at homeless shelters. In small group meetings, they share joys and struggles, pray together, and encourage each other. They build one another up with love and service, creating a safe space where everyone belongs.

To truly accept this new life, you need to roll up your sleeves and dive into the work. Building the body of Christ requires each of us to step up and offer our gifts and callings. If we all pitch in, what emerges is nothing short of beautiful. We will have a spiritual temple glowing with the love and grace of God. Paul urged the Corinthians to "excel in building up the church" (1 Corinthians 14:12). That call is ours too.

The destruction of the old temple signifies a tearing down of outdated religious systems and mindsets, replaced by the new spiritual temple found in Christ. This change leads to something far greater: a new covenant rooted in love, faith, and unity. What old beliefs do you need to let go of to fully embrace your identity in Christ? Are you willing to break free of what's holding you back and step into the new life Jesus offers?

In order to be turned into a component of the living temple that is blazing brightly for the New Kingdom, here is the task and the hope that you should take on.

Chapter 5: Being Born Again: the renovation of the inner build

"So God created mankind in his own image, in the image of God he created them; male and female he created them."

-Genesis 1:27

In Genesis, God lovingly created us to mirror His character. He wanted us to show the world mercy and love. Something we would want other people to show to us. Through being born again, we are given a chance to embrace this original design once more. It is not simply a religious ritual or surface-level change but a complete renewal of the heart, mind, and spirit. When we have absolute faith in Jesus and the power of the Holy Spirit, we are invited to step into this new life and live fully as God's redeemed children.

This verse from Genesis reminds us of the precious image God intended for humanity from the very beginning. We were meant to reflect His nature in the world, living in perfect harmony with Him and with each other. However, the tragic fall of humanity in the Garden of Eden marred that original design, separating us from God and leaving us with a fractured relationship.

Do you think God won't have a plan? Do you think He would leave us? But God's plan of redemption through Jesus Christ allows us to be born again and restored to our original purpose.

In John 3, we see Jesus explaining this process to Nicodemus, a respected religious leader who struggled to understand what Jesus meant by being "born again." Jesus said to him, *"Very truly*

I tell you, no one can see the Kingdom of God unless they are born again" (John 3:3). Nicodemus was puzzled and asked how one could be born a second time if they had already been born of their mother. Jesus then explains that this new birth is not physical but spiritual, brought about by the Holy Spirit.

Here, this concept of being born again is central to Christianity. It speaks to a complete transformation—a rebirth into a new life through Christ. When we accept Jesus as our Savior, the Holy Spirit renews us from the inside out. This renewal is not about modifying external behaviors but about transitioning from the old life of sin to a new life of freedom in Christ. It's about restoring the image God intended for us in Genesis 1:27, where we can live in harmony with Him and reflect His goodness.

Spiritually, this rebirth means letting go of past sins and seeking God's transformative power to cleanse and renew us. Like Nicodemus, we may not understand the full extent of what God intends, but through faith and surrender to the Spirit, we can become new creations (2 Corinthians 5:17). This renewal is accomplished through faith in Jesus and the indwelling work of the Holy Spirit.

The Apostle Paul further shed light on this transformation, emphasizing that in this new life, there is no condemnation for those who are in Christ (Romans 8:1). The Holy Spirit convicts us of sin, points us toward righteousness, and reminds us of our standing as God's children. Being born again means surrendering our old lives of sin, striving to live according to the principles of God's Kingdom, and ultimately being reconciled to the Creator who fashioned us in His image.

As believers, this new birth calls us to see ourselves as God sees us—beloved, forgiven, and purposed for good works. We receive a new identity not rooted in human standards but in our standing before God. To be able to understand the symbolic and spiritual implications of this rebirth, it challenges us to examine our lives, letting the Holy Spirit reveal areas that need renewal and change.

Inner Renewal through the Holy Spirit

Have you ever felt a fire ignite deep within you, a yearning for something more? That's the Holy Spirit stirring your soul, the inner renewal of a believer – a heart-pounding, life-altering transformation! No mere tinkering; this is a glorious renovation orchestrated by the Holy Spirit himself.

He's not here with a paintbrush for touch-ups; He's wielding the power of God to break down the walls of your old self and rebuild them in the image of your Creator. It all starts with a gentle nudge, a conviction that awakens you to the truth. Like a best friend who loves you fiercely, the Holy Spirit whispers about the areas where you can truly blossom. He doesn't shame, he doesn't judge, he simply shows you the path to a life overflowing with God's love.

This inner renewal is a thrilling adventure, a chance to shed the burdens that hold you back and embrace the magnificent plan God has in store. It's a wave of emotion washing over you, a cleansing fire purging away negativity, and a surge of strength empowering you to become the person you were always meant to be. It's a love story unfolding within you, a breathtaking transformation that will leave you breathless with awe.

Are you ready to answer the call?

Once conviction takes root, cleansing begins. The Spirit cleanses us through the redemptive work of Jesus Christ, washing away guilt and offering us forgiveness. We all have experienced moments where we regret our words or actions, but the Holy Spirit helps us understand that no mistake is beyond redemption. He takes our deepest shame and replaces it with freedom and a renewed sense of purpose.

The Holy Spirit gives us the strength to live out this new identity as this internal restoration takes place. This empowerment is a deep, persistent conviction that God is working in and through us to accomplish His objectives, not merely a fleeting energy boost. In Ephesians 3:16–17, Paul aptly expresses, *"I pray that out of His glorious riches, He may strengthen you with power through His Spirit in your inner being, so that Christ may dwell in your hearts by faith."*

What if you came across the most beautiful garden you've ever seen, overflowing with vibrant fruits – love so sweet it fills your heart to burst—a joy that bubbles up like a hidden spring, the peace that settles like a gentle snowfall? These aren't just fruits; they're living proof that the Holy Spirit is working within you!

They're not grown by willpower alone but by the miraculous touch of God. When you see someone radiate patience in a raging storm or offer kindness to an empty well, that's the Spirit's light shining through. It's a breathtaking transformation, a masterpiece painted on the canvas of your soul.

Life throws punches, doesn't it? We teeter on the edge of burnout, our patience frays, and sometimes darkness threatens to engulf us. But in those moments, the Holy Spirit whispers, "Don't you worry, child. I'm your wellspring, your never-ending river of strength." He recharges your weary heart, reminding you of God's love.

Trusting the Spirit is like holding onto a guiding star on the stormiest night. It means immersing yourself in prayer, letting scripture be your map, and surrounding yourself with a community that lifts you up. It's about surrendering your anxieties, knowing He'll lead you to the calm after the storm. This is more than just a journey; it's an adventure, a love story written between your soul and the Divine.

Renewing the Mind and Heart

Changing the old ways of thinking is very important for every Christian to live out the new identity that Christ has given them. We have to reflect on the Apostle's words and see how they urged us. *"Be transformed by the renewing of your mind" (Romans 12:2).* Here, they reminded us that our thoughts and attitudes shape our actions. Without a change in mindset, our old habits will continue to steer us away from God's purposes. Only when we align our thoughts with His will will we begin to truly see ourselves and the world differently and experience true transformation.

The process of renewing the mind begins with recognizing which thought patterns need to change. Have you noticed those recurring thoughts that keep you stuck in fear, shame, or bitterness? Maybe it's the belief that you aren't good enough or that past failures define your future. These thoughts can be like heavy chains, restricting our spiritual growth. Only when we engage ourselves in deep prayer and reflect fervently on Scripture are we able to escape these harmful cycles.

In prayer, we surrender our minds to God, inviting Him to reshape our thinking. Prayer is more than a list of requests; it's an intimate conversation that allows us to lay our burdens before God and listen to His voice. When we take time to be still in His presence, our hearts soften, and our minds become receptive to His truth.

Scripture meditation is another important exercise that needs to be done in order to rejuvenate the mind. The Bible is not merely a collection of ancient teachings; rather, it is a living, breathing guide that addresses our most profound challenges in a comprehensive manner. We are able to replace the lies of the world with the promises of God when we immerse ourselves in its truths. As an illustration, the Bible encourages you to "cast all your anxiety on Him because He cares for you" (1 Peter 5:7) whenever you are experiencing feelings of being overwhelmed and overcome with anxiety. The shift in this emphasis can transform hopelessness into optimism and fear into faith.

For renewing our thoughts and hearts, fellowship with other Christians is just as important. Encouragement, accountability, and counsel that are applicable to our lives are all things that we obtain when we surround ourselves with a community that shares our beliefs. When you were with a reliable buddy, have you ever had a talk that inspired or uplifted you? Conversations like these cannot only push us to see things in a fresh light but also break down boundaries and drive us to move forward in our faith.

Additionally, humility, appreciation, and faith are required in order to cultivate a mindset that is centered on Christ. We are reminded by humility that we are unable to alter ourselves and that we require the grace of God in order to change. It implies being aware of our shortcomings and being willing to work on improving ourselves and growing as individuals. When we are grateful, our attention is shifted from what we do not have to what God has already provided for us. When we cultivate an attitude of gratitude, we can nurture a glad heart that acknowledges the goodness of God. There is something to be thankful for in every circumstance one may find themselves in. The practice of faith requires us to have faith in God's plan, even when we are unable to see the way forward. It is the conviction that God is directing our lives toward a future that is rich in meaning and that He is working everything out for our benefit.

What steps can we take today to renew our minds and hearts? It starts with recognizing the lies that hold us back and replacing them with God's truth. It means spending time in prayer, immersing ourselves in Scripture, and surrounding ourselves with a community that will encourage us. It means choosing humility, gratitude, and faith, trusting that God is in control. As our thoughts align with God's will, our hearts will follow, and we will be transformed to reflect the character of Christ more and more each day.

Overcoming Old Habits and Patterns

Living out our purpose in Christ requires us to break free from old habits and patterns that impede spiritual progress. For a great number of Christians, these damaging tendencies act as bonds that keep us from fully experiencing God's love and purpose. They consist of things like addiction, unforgiveness, and pessimism. However, there is good news: God's grace is more than enough to actually transform our lives for the better.

One of the most prevalent habits that might hinder us is unforgiveness. We should naturally feel resentment and hatred toward someone who has badly wronged us. But holding onto those emotions might turn into a prison that keeps us mired in resentment. Perhaps a close friend or family member has harmed you, and the hurt seems unbreakable. Even though you may feel justified in clinging to it, the only person you can actually hurt by being unforgiving is yourself. Christ asks us to provide forgiveness, just as He did, not because we think the other person merits it but rather because it frees us and brings us tranquility.

Addiction is just another unhealthy habit that impedes our development. An unhealthy relationship with food, drugs, pornography, or social media is just one example of how addictions may take hold and overwhelm us, making it difficult for us to concentrate on the really important things. However, hope remains. Our challenges do not determine the extent of God's grace. His love is able to enter our deepest moments and bring us to light. Admitting our shortcomings to others and asking for support from dependable friends or experts are common steps in recovery. We can have the bravery to rebel in a nurturing setting.

Negative thinking is just like like unforgiveness and addiction. It can be deeply ingrained in our minds. The constant doubts and worries can seem like a soundtrack playing over and over, convincing us that we're not good enough, smart enough, or worthy enough.

It's easy to feel hopeless when this negativity shapes our self-perception. Then there is God, who saves us and calls us to renew our minds to believe in the truth that we are wonderfully made, valued, and loved. To overcome such negative thinking, we need to start by recognizing our lies and replacing them with God's truth.

Confession, accountability, and perseverance are key to overcoming these patterns. Confession is the first step. When we bring our struggles into the light, we strip them of their power and open ourselves up to healing. The Bible says, *"Confess your sins to each other and pray for each other so that you may be healed."* - James 5:16.

Sharing our burdens with a trusted friend or mentor helps us to stop carrying them alone.

Accountability is equally important. It comes after confession and fully accepting that 'yes,' you are a human aand have made the mistake of overstepping the bounds. Surround yourself with people who will walk alongside you, celebrate your victories, and gently challenge you when you stray. This kind of support network will provide strength and encouragement as you journey toward freedom.

Perseverance is the final ingredient. It is the most important aspect of overcoming old habits, and let me tell you, it is not easy at all. Some days will be filled with joy and progress, and others will feel like two steps backward. Don't give up on the hope that God's grace will carry you through. He who began a good work in you will see it through to completion (Philippians 1:6). Don't let the setbacks make you believe the journey isn't worth it.

You have to self-reflect at times to the teachings and remember that real change is possible through God's grace. Let this truth be your anchor: God's love never fails. No habit or pattern is too strong for Him to break. So, whatever chains are holding you back today, know that you can be free. Confess your struggles, seek accountability, and persevere with hope. A new life is waiting for you—a life filled with joy, peace, and a renewed purpose.

Living Out the New Identity in Christ

When we accept the new paths in the adventures of Christ and fully accept our new image through rebirth, we step into a reality that transcends our former limitations. The Bible reminds us that we are no longer slaves to sin or bound by our old ways.

Instead, as believers, we are children of God, co-heirs with Christ, and members of a royal priesthood. But what does it mean to live out this identity each day? How do we practically embody our new calling?

First, let's reflect on what it means to be a child of God. In John 1:12, we read that *"to all who did receive Him, to those who believed in His name, He gave the right to become children of God."* This relationship is more deep than mere acknowledgment. As children of God, we are cherished, protected, and guided. Do you recognize that you have the privilege of calling the Creator of the universe your Father? You belong in His family, unconditionally loved and accepted.

As co-heirs with Christ, we share in the inheritance of eternal life and the promise of God's Kingdom. What an amazing reality that we can boldly approach God's throne, not as distant subjects but as beloved children. We are also part of a royal priesthood, called to reflect God's light in the world. This means representing God's love and mercy to those who haven't yet experienced His grace.

Living out our identity in Christ means cultivating kindness, generosity, and the boldness to share the gospel with others. In practical terms, kindness means treating people with gentleness and compassion, even those who may not reciprocate. This could look like listening patiently to someone who feels unheard or offering help without expecting anything in return. A single act of kindness, like encouraging a discouraged co-worker or providing a meal to a grieving neighbor, can bring hope where despair once lingered.

Generosity should naturally flow from our new identity. When we recognize that everything we have comes from God, we give freely, knowing He will provide for our needs. Generosity isn't only about finances—it can include sharing time and skills or even just offering a smile to brighten someone's day. When we give without hesitation or reservation, we reflect God's abundant love.

Sharing the gospel is another powerful expression of our new identity. It's time to stop being hesitant to speak about our faith with someone, fearing judgment or rejection. If we truly believe that Christ's love has transformed our lives, why would we keep this gift to ourselves? Living out the gospel might mean inviting a neighbor to church, sharing your testimony over coffee, or simply praying for someone in need.

Each of us is uniquely equipped with gifts and talents to serve and glorify God. Are you an encourager, organizer, musician, or caregiver? These strengths are not coincidental but are meant to be used boldly for God's purposes. You need to stop and reflect on how you can step more fully into your calling today, whether it's serving your church, mentoring someone, or building bridges across different communities.

When you offer your many gifts to God, it can transform lives and bring hope.

So stop and ask yourself. How am I embodying my identity as a child of God, a co-heir with Christ, and a member of a royal priesthood? How can I intentionally practice kindness and generosity and share the gospel in my daily life? Most importantly, how will I step boldly into my calling, using my unique gifts to serve and glorify God?

The answers lie in your journey of faith and the joy of knowing who you truly are in Christ. Embrace this identity daily, knowing that in Him, you have all the strength and courage to live fully and make a difference in the world.

Chapter 6: The Death, Burial, and Resurrection of Jesus

"And I will put enmity between you and the woman, and between your offspring and her offspring; he shall bruise your head, and you shall bruise his heel."

-Genesis 3:15

Since the very start, from the dawn of human history, God has formulated a basis for redemption. He dictated a narrative, so rich and beautiful, filled with promises and fulfillment, that it left everyone in awe. Consider the words of Genesis above, and notice how beautifully these words are spoken by God in the aftermath of humanity's first disobedience. It sets a stage not just for the conflict of ages but for the ultimate victory of Christ over Satan, sin, and death.

This verse carries the weight of God's eternal plan for salvation. It surely is a mystery that reveals through the ages, culminating in the life, death, and resurrection of Jesus Christ.

Why is this ancient promise needed by believers? And how does Christ's victory resonate with us today in our everyday struggles and pain?

In the battle between good and evil, Jesus' death on the cross might seem, at first glance, like a moment of defeat. Satan bruised His heel—a wound, albeit painful and significant. Even then, this 'apparent' defeat was precisely the act through which Jesus crushed the serpent's head, a fatal blow defeating the powers of darkness. This is the paradox at the heart of the

Christian faith: we are to get victory through apparent defeat, strength in weakness, and life through death.

Isn't it astounding how God turns what looks like the end into a glorious new beginning?

Take a moment to consider the impact this victory would have. Jesus' resurrection is the ultimate demonstration of God's power over sin and death. It is not merely a historical event but a pivotal moment that changes everything. Because He lives, we, too, can live with the hope of eternal life. This is the promise of redemption fulfilled, the assurance that no matter the depth of darkness we face, the light of Christ prevails.

This ancient victory has such a magnanimous effect that it also affects us in the modern world. Every day, we face our own battles with sin and temptation. We encounter the brokenness of the world in vivid ways, and in that, we fight our inner weaknesses as well. We do this through strained relationships, personal failures, or the pain of loss and keep on going with the hope given to us by Jesus and His words.

In these moments, can we see Jesus' victory as our own? Can we hold onto hope when despair seems justifiable?

The answer lies in our connectedness to Christ. Just as Jesus overcame, so too can we, through Him, overcome the trials we face. That is our hope right there. The resurrection power that raised Christ from the dead is the same power that lives in every believer. This means that in every moment of weakness and every instance of doubt, we have access to divine strength and victory.

Here, we really need to stop and ask ourselves: Do we live in the light of Christ's victory? Are our lives a demonstration of the power of His resurrection? We need not be the people who see but do not perceive. We have to allow our faith to be active, our hope vibrant, and our love to reflect the One who loved us first.

Fighting through the complexities of life, let our hearts be anchored in this truth: the battle is already won, and the victory is ours in Christ. With every challenge we face, may we remember that because He lives, we too shall live and not just survive but thrive.

The Necessity of Jesus' Death

Why did Jesus have to die?

Time and time again, we ask this question to ourselves and to the ones who claim to know the word of god closely. It's a question that has echoed through the corridors of time by various people of faith and even those who lie outside the bounds of our religion. For some, the truth touched their hearts sooner rather than later and stirred deep reflections on the nature of sacrifice and redemption.

At the heart of Christianity, we succumb to a great mystery: the Son of God came to earth, not to conquer with might but to redeem through suffering, not to inflict punishment but to bear it, not to rule in arrogance but to serve in humility—and ultimately, to die on a cross.

The concept of atonement is that God reconciles the world to Himself through Christ's sacrifice. This runs deep through the scriptures and finds its roots in the Old Testament. Every lamb sacrificed on the altar, every offering made for sins, was a foreshadowing of the One who would come to fulfill all righteousness. Jesus' death was prefigured in these Old Testament sacrifices, each one a poignant reminder that without the shedding of blood, there is no forgiveness of sins (Hebrews 9:22).

The Passover lamb emerges as a compelling figure when we see the inner folds of Bible typology. It is immaculate and willingly offered; its blood daubed on the doorframes served as a potent symbol for the Israelites, heralding their deliverance from the looming specter of death in Egypt. This ancient ritual is steeped in faith and obedience and prefigures a more philosophical salvation narrative.

Now, take the monumental sacrifice of Christ, the quintessential Lamb of God, into perspective. Unlike any other, His sacrifice is both necessary and overpoweringly sufficient for our ultimate redemption from the shackles of sin and the finality of death.

The moment of His death on the cross is nothing short of a cosmic upheaval. It is a veil in the temple, that thick, imposing fabric symbolizing the separation between the divine and the mortal, was torn asunder from top to bottom. This act was far from mere symbolism; it signified the dramatic conclusion of the old covenant, an era where access to God was mediated through priests and a litany of sacrifices. In its place, a new covenant was unfurled—a covenant characterized by a direct, unmediated relationship with God, made possible through the ultimate sacrifice of Jesus Christ. This pivotal moment in history marks the transition from a faith of outward rituals to a faith of inward transformation, inviting all into an intimate, personal communion with the Divine.

But why death? Could there not have been another way?

Here lies the depth of God's love for us. It is a love so deep that it chose to suffer in our place. Jesus' death was not just an act of love but the culmination of divine justice meeting divine mercy. We were estranged, lost, and deserving of the wages of our sins, which is death. Then, through His death, Jesus took upon Himself what was ours and gave us what His—righteousness and life were.

Think about the times you've felt the weight of guilt or shame, the times you've longed for forgiveness and a fresh start. In our human relationships, we see that true reconciliation often involves profound personal costs. Someone forgives a debt; someone absorbs the pain of betrayal without retaliating. How much greater, then, is the reconciliation brought about by Jesus' death, which restores our broken relationship with God?

Jesus' invitation to take up our cross and follow Him (Matthew 16:24) is not just a call to bear burdens but a call to enter into the life He offers through His death—a life of freedom, purpose, and hope.

Are we really ready to accept this gift? Are we prepared to live in the freedom purchased at such a great price?

Reflecting on the necessity of His death, let it not just be a theological assent but an emotional engagement with the reality of what His sacrifice means.

Well, it means everything for us. And it continues to be the main essence of why we live and how we live.

The Symbolism of Burial

In the quiet halls of the tomb, where the silence echoes through the tombs with faithful whispers of life that seem to fade from afar, the burial of Jesus Christ holds eccentric symbolism and deep significance. To understand the emotional and spiritual weight of this event, we must really get into what it represents—not just as a historical act but as a transformative element of the Christian faith.

Jesus' burial was the tipping point. Why? Well, the full human experience of death encapsulated and highlighted the reality of His incarnation. Christ was not a disembodied spirit. He was a human! He was flesh and blood, who breathed, walked, wept, and ultimately died!

His burial in the tomb accentuates His complete identification with the human condition, that he was a living and breathing mortal who gave His life for us. He knowingly stepped onto the altar, knowing his life would end and would not continue beyond that day in the human world. It tells us that the Son of God was willing to embrace the entirety of human suffering, including its ultimate consequence—death. But why does this matter?

Do you understand the full capacity we have we actually lost? Take into consideration the people we've lost, the graves we've stood before, and the impending sense of finality that accompanies each farewell. Death is a universal experience, an inevitable end that every person must face. In laying His body to rest, Jesus shared in this universal human narrative, yet without sin. His burial is a stark reminder that He truly was 'a man of sorrows and acquainted with grief' (Isaiah 53:3). But more than that, it shows that He was willing to take the full measure of human brokenness upon Himself.

But the tomb was not just about death; it also symbolized a period of waiting and the promise of new life. For the disciples, the days following Jesus' burial were filled with confusion and mourning. In fact, this period of waiting was pregnant with purpose. It was a divine pause, filled with anticipation for the resurrection morning. This waiting mirrors so many of our own experiences—the in-between times when hope seems dim, and the promise of change or healing feels distant.

In our lives, we, too, experience these 'tomb' phases—periods of uncertainty, despair, or transition. We lay dreams, relationships, or plans to rest, not knowing what will emerge from these times of waiting. Yet, the story of Jesus' burial and resurrection invites us to view these tomb-like experiences differently. They are not the end but a preparation for something new, a space where hope can take root and flourish.

What does this mean for us, then?

The tomb signifies that out of our deepest despairs and endings can come profound new beginnings. Just as Jesus emerged from the grave in resurrected glory, our most challenging times can lead to new growth and unforeseen pathways. The resurrection power that raised Christ from the dead is the same power available to us today, offering us hope and new life.

As we reflect on the symbolism of Jesus' burial, let us ask ourselves: Where are we experiencing tomb-like situations in our own lives? Are we allowing these periods to be fertile ground for God's transformation? Or are we losing hope in the waiting?

The same God who raised Jesus from the dead is at work in us. He can bring light out of darkness and life out of death just as the tomb could not hold Jesus; our circumstances, no matter how dire, are not the end of our story. With God, there is always a promise of new life, a hope that does not disappoint.

The Power of the Resurrection

The resurrection of Jesus Christ is not merely a historical footnote or a symbolic anecdote—it is the cornerstone of the Christian faith, imbued with weighted implications for theology and the life of every believer. It's the triumph of life over death, light over darkness, grace over sin. But what does this mean for us today? How does this ancient miracle transform our modern lives?

Here, we need to understand that the resurrection validates everything Jesus claimed about Himself—His divinity, His role as the Messiah, and His power over death. This affirmation is crucial; it means that His teachings are not just wise words from a spiritual leader but the living truth from the Son of God. This truth holds the power to change lives, mend what's broken, and restore what was lost.

Life can feel like a relentless storm, wave after wave, leaving you battered and breathless. You wonder if there's even a point to clinging on if the next blow will finally be the one to drown you. Maybe you've lost someone you loved, or maybe it's just the weight of the world that's got you questioning everything.

Hope seems like a distant memory, a flickering candle in a hurricane. But then you remember. Remember the story, the one that has anchored countless souls for centuries. The story of Jesus, broken and bleeding, laid in a tomb. With all odds against Him, he emerged alive.

Death, the ultimate thief, was defeated.

That, my friend, is more than just a story. It's a life raft in the stormiest sea. It's the promise that no matter how dark things get or how heavy the burden is, there is always a way out. Because if Jesus, the Son of God, could conquer death, then surely we can weather any storm life throws our way!

The resurrection isn't a guarantee of smooth sailing. There will still be challenges; there will still be hurdles whose load is impossible to bear. But it's the promise that we are not alone in this fight. It's the fuel that reignites the fire of hope, the whisper that says, 'Get up. You are not done yet.'

The resurrection also fundamentally alters our understanding of life and death. Death is no longer an end but a transition, a doorway to eternal life with Christ. This perspective can radically change how we live our day-to-day lives—how we value our time, how we treat others, and how we prioritize our commitments. Knowing that our physical death is not the final word inspires us to live more purposefully and invest in things with eternal significance rather than transient value.

Have you ever felt stuck in a cycle of mess-ups? Do you keep tripping over the same mistakes, weighed down by the baggage of your past? The kind of feeling that makes you wonder if you'll ever break free?

Well, the resurrection of Jesus flips that script entirely. It's not just about Jesus coming back to life; it's about us being born again. Imagine that! Mind you, not by our own power, but by the amazing grace of God working through the Holy Spirit.

We need to think of the ways of John Newton, who was a slave trader who wrote 'Amazing Grace.' Talk about a turnaround! After embracing Jesus' message, he became an abolitionist, fighting against the very evil he once participated in. That's the power of the resurrection—it doesn't hold your past against you. It offers a clean slate, a chance to walk a brand new path.

Those deepest regrets, the worst things you've done or have thought of doing, the mere specks in the otherwise clear sky should not have the power to define you anymore. The resurrection is like God saying, 'Hey, it's not over. You can start fresh. You can be better.' It's a powerful truth, a lifeline for anyone who feels lost or beyond redemption. No matter how far you feel you've strayed, there's always a way back to God's light.

Through this, believers are given additional ability to act as agents of change in the world. The broken, the lost, and the hurting are the recipients of the message of hope that we are commanded to deliver. In a world that is in dire need of peacemakers, healers, and messengers of good news, it inspires us to be those who bring about changes for the better. Every single act of kindness, every single gesture of love, and every single word of truth that we proclaim is a rippling effect of the power of the resurrection that is at work in our lives.

The question that we should ask ourselves when we take the time to contemplate the transformative power of the resurrection is, 'How are we living out this new life?' Which of the freedoms and powers that the resurrection bestows upon us are we currently experiencing? What changes are we making in our lives that will have an effect on other people?

In the lives of all those who have faith, the resurrection is not merely a past occurrence or a promise for the future; rather, it is a present reality that is alive and active. Therefore, let us not live as people who believe in the tomb but rather as people who believe in the resurrection, and let us loudly announce that since He lives, we, too, are able to genuinely live.

Living in the Reality of the Resurrection

Living in the light of the resurrection of Jesus is not merely a spiritual concept that could be contemplated; rather, it is a reality that has the potential to transform our lives and should permeate every part of our lives. The question is, how can we, as believers, make use of this amazing ability on a daily basis? Our approach to the hardships and tribulations we endure, the sins we strive against, and our journey of spiritual growth is altered in what ways as a result of this.

Death. Just this one word has the power to send shivers down any person's spine. Maybe you're facing a health scare yourself, or someone you love is battling a tough illness. It's enough to make you want to crawl under the covers and shut the world out.

But here's the thing most of us forget: death doesn't win. Not in the end. The resurrection of Jesus is the ultimate underdog story. He beat the unbeatable. And that changes everything.

For a believer facing a storm-like sickness, the resurrection isn't a guarantee of earthly healing, but it's a promise of something far greater. It's the knowledge that even if your body weakens here, there's an eternity waiting on the other side—an eternity without pain, doctors, or goodbyes. It's a peace that passes all understanding.

This hope doesn't make the fight any easier, mind you. You still take your meds; you still fight for every good day. But it changes your perspective. Because win or lose here, you know you've already won the ultimate battle.

That victory spills over into everything else, too. See, the resurrection isn't just about conquering death; it's about conquering the stuff that drags us down every day—the lies, the grudges, the things that keep us from being the best versions of ourselves.

Don't we all want to live in a world where forgiveness is easier than holding a grudge, where honesty is the default, not the exception? That's the kind of life the resurrection makes possible. Every choice you make to be that kind of person, to fight for what's right, is a way of living out the victory Jesus won for you. It's a way of saying death won't win, not today, not ever.

The actuality of the resurrection also has a significant impact on the development of one's spirituality. Our metamorphosis from who we were to who we are becoming in Christ is fueled by this, and it is who we are becoming. In the same way that Jesus rose from the dead, we are also raised from our previous ways and brought into a new life filled with a deep connection with God and a vivid faith. This can be observed in the believer who spends their mornings in prayer and scripture, finding the courage to face the challenges of the day with grace and knowledge in each verse that they read.

Every dawn is a reminder of the triumph that Jesus won, and every decision is an opportunity to exhibit that power in our lives. This is what it means to live in the reality of the resurrection. With that in mind, let us ask ourselves: Are we walking as persons who have been transformed by this truth? What steps might we take to more fully embody the power of resurrection in each and every day?

As we reflect on the significant implications of Jesus' death, burial, and resurrection, we are called not just to ponder these truths but to live them out actively. These elements of Christ's life are not just historical facts to be admired from a distance; they are transformative realities meant to impact our lives deeply.

At the start of the chapter, Genesis 3:15 promises a beautifully fulfilled victory in Jesus, reminding us that each day is an opportunity to experience the resurrection power.

In his book *Mere Christianity*, C.S. Lewis writes, 'If you read history, you will find that the Christians who did most for the present world were precisely those who thought most of the next.' This call to action challenges us to live not as passive observers waiting for eternity but as vibrant participants experiencing and manifesting the resurrection power here and now.

As believers, we are sanctioned to live boldly, love radically, and serve passionately, demonstrating the transformative power of the resurrection in every aspect of our lives. Let us then step forward, motivated by Christ's victory, to impact our world, knowing that the power that raised Jesus from the dead is at work within us, calling us to higher purposes and greater joys.

Chapter 7: The Temple of God Completed

"Thus the heavens and the earth were completed in all their vast array."

- Genesis 2:1

The completion of the Temple of God, as foretold through Scripture, holds the main foundation for the believers to stand united in Christ and safeguard their faith. When we consider the expansive creation of the universe, which is also highlighted in the scripture above, we see a universe finished in all its complex and wonderful detail. It is but a direct reflection of God's sovereignty and intentionality. This act of completion not only showcased God's unmatched power but also set the stage for His ongoing work in the spiritual realm. This is particularly found in the lives of those who follow Christ.

When we take the physical world into perspective, the completion of the heavens and the earth here marks the beginning of humanity's journey within God's perfect creation. In the same way, on the spiritual side, the completion of the Temple of God signifies a fundamental moment in the divine narrative. It is a moment where the spiritual maturity and unity of believers culminate in a living, breathing testimony to God's ongoing work on Earth.

This spiritual temple isn't made of stone or mortar; instead, it is built from the lives of believers, cemented together by faith, and crowned with the presence of Christ Himself. Just as the physical temple in Jerusalem was considered God's dwelling place, so too are the hearts of believers now the place where His Spirit resides. The proponent Paul highlights this beautifully in 1 Corinthians 3:16, where he asks, *"Do you not know that you are God's temple and that God's Spirit dwells in you?"*

The completion of this spiritual temple is definitely going to have implications of all kinds.

The most important thing would be that it would represent the fulfillment of God's promise to dwell among His people, to live and prosper WITH them. This is a promise that spans from the Old Testament tabernacle and temple to the indwelling presence of the Holy Spirit today. The temple's completion is not just a theological concept but a reality that affects how we live, worship, and interact with the world around us.

For believers, being part of this completed temple means living lives that reflect the holiness and love of God. It means that our actions, our decisions, and our words are bricks in the edifice of God's living temple, each one essential and purposeful. It challenges us to live intentionally, understanding that our lives are not just our own but are integral parts of a divine structure designed to bring glory to God and light to the world.

Moreover, the completion of God's temple heralds a new era of spiritual unity and collective mission. In a world fractured by division, the church stands as a testament to God's plan for a unified body of believers, transcending cultural, racial, and economic barriers. This unity is not superficial; it is rooted in the deepest truths of the gospel, calling for sacrificial love and mutual edification.

In practical terms, living as part of this completed temple means engaging in acts of worship not just inside church walls but in every context of our lives. It means service that extends beyond comfort zones and prayers that reach beyond personal needs. It involves a community of believers who support, challenge, and nurture one another towards spiritual maturity and Christlikeness.

How are we contributing to this divine edifice? Are our lives reflecting the holiness and love that are expected of God's temple? This perspective shifts our daily living from mundane routine to divine mission, imbuing our simplest actions with eternal purpose. Let us then live not as isolated believers but as integral parts of this grand, divine temple that God is completing in and through us.

The Biblical Blueprint of the Spiritual Temple

The very foundation of our faith, the New Testament, is not mere words on a page; it's a divinely crafted blueprint, a map to the glorious spiritual temple – and guess who the cornerstone is?

That's right, our Lord and Savior, Jesus Christ himself!

This temple is a spiritual edifice and not just a dwelling place for the Holy Spirit himself!

And how do we know this? Because Jesus himself told us! Remember the story of the temple in Jerusalem? When those blind fools wanted to tear it down, Jesus declared, *"Destroy this temple, and in three days, I will raise it up!"* They thought he was talking about bricks and beams, though He was talking about something far greater, a purpose that he would fulfill with his own body!

Jesus, in his infinite wisdom, was analytical enough to highlight his glorious resurrection all this time! He was the sacrifice, the lamb upon the altar, and his rising from the dead was the ultimate act that established this new spiritual temple—a temple not confined by walls but built within the hearts of all true believers!

So, when the trumpets will blare, the choirs will then sing! Let the heavens rejoice, for the King has conquered death and built a temple for his followers, a temple that will stand for eternity!

Why does this matter? The resurrection of Jesus is the cornerstone of our faith and the spiritual temple. It signifies that the temple is not confined to a location but is a living, breathing entity animated by Christ Himself. This shifts our understanding from observing religious rituals in a designated holy place to living out our faith in a dynamic, global, and personal context. Jesus' resurrection assures us that God's presence is no longer localized to a specific geographic location but is accessible to all who believe in Him, anywhere and at any time.

Another significant instant was when Jesus drove out the money changers from the temple (Matthew 21:12-13). He declared outrightly, *"My house shall be called a house of prayer, but you make it a den of robbers."* Jesus reclaims the temple as a place of spiritual integrity and focus. This act not only cleanses the physical temple but also points to the purity and devotion expected in the spiritual temple, which is the collective body of believers. It calls us to remove anything in our lives that corrupts or hinders our relationship with God.

We contribute to the completion of this spiritual temple by living out the truth of the gospel. We do this by embodying the love, grace, and holiness that Jesus demonstrated. Each act of kindness, each moment of genuine worship, and each decision to forsake sin builds up the temple. For example, when a believer chooses to forgive instead of harboring bitterness, they align themselves with the cornerstone—Christ—and his teachings. They become a living stone in this spiritual edifice, promoting unity and embodying the gospel's transformative power.

Here, I would urge the readers to imagine a giant mosaic where each tile is unique and beautiful in its own way. We need to notice that these tiles all *work* together, and in that cohesion, they can create a breathtaking masterpiece. That's how the Bible describes the spiritual temple—a community of believers where everyone contributes their strengths and talents.

We're not just disconnected individuals going through life alone. We're all part of something bigger that transcends our little stories. Each person has a special role to play, like a specific tile in the mosaic. When one piece is cracked or weak in a building, it affects the whole structure – our religion is the same.

That's why it's so important to focus on our own spiritual growth. It's not just about ourselves; it's about being the strongest, most positive version of ourselves for the sake of the entire community. When we're healthy and growing in our faith, we create a safe space for others to find peace, connect with God, and feel supported.

The next time you feel like your faith is small or insignificant, remember – you're a vital piece of a much bigger picture. We're all working together on this incredible, eternal project, building a spiritual temple that will leave a lasting impact on the world.

The Role of Believers in Building the Temple

As followers of Christ, we are not mere spectators in the narrative of faith; we are active participants, called to be 'living stones' in the construction of a spiritual temple, as beautifully metaphorized in 1 Peter 2:5.

Each believer, infused with the breath of life through the Holy Spirit, contributes uniquely and essentially to this divine structure. What does this mean for us, and how do we embody such a profound calling in our everyday lives?

Living in the light of the resurrection of Jesus is not merely a spiritual concept that could be contemplated; rather, it is a reality that has the potential to transform our lives and should permeate every part of our lives. The question is, how can we, as believers, make use of this amazing ability on a daily basis? Our approach to the hardships and tribulations we endure, the sins we strive against, and our journey of spiritual growth is altered in what ways as a result of this.

You should think about the great hope that comes from knowing that death has been defeated. It is expected that this reassurance will change how we deal with the problems and fears we face every day. For example, the promise of the resurrection can bring a lot of peace and strength to a believer who is sick with a dangerous illness. Also, it's not just the promise of healing; it's also the deeper promise of eternal life and a future without pain or sorrow. Not only does this hope give people a new reason to fight, but it also gives them hope that they will succeed in some way.

In addition, the force of the resurrection has an impact on our fight against moral decay. Being aware of the fact that Christ triumphed over death gives us the strength to triumph over the sins that entangle us. For it is not enough to simply abstain from engaging in wrongdoing; rather, it is necessary to embrace a life of righteousness made possible by Jesus Christ's resurrection. Choosing to be honest in an environment that favors dishonesty or forgiving someone when it is simpler to hold a grudge are two examples of acts that could be considered examples of this. Every decision you make is a step towards living the life that has been revived.

The actuality of the resurrection also has a significant impact on the development of one's spirituality. Our metamorphosis from who we were to who we are becoming in Christ is fueled by this, and it is who we are becoming. In the same manner that Jesus was risen from the dead, we are also raised from our previous ways and brought into a new life that is filled with a deep connection with God and a vivid faith. This can be observed in the believer who spends their mornings in prayer and scripture, finding the courage to face the challenges of the day with grace and knowledge in each verse that they read.

Every dawn is a reminder of the triumph that Jesus won, and every decision is an opportunity to exhibit that power in our lives. This is what it means to live in the reality of the resurrection. With that in mind, let us ask ourselves: Are we walking as persons whom this truth has transformed? What steps might we take to more fully embody the power of resurrection in each and every day? Rather than merely being questions for contemplation, these are summons to action, challenging us to live our lives not as people who are waiting for the resurrection to occur someday but rather as individuals who are experiencing the power of the resurrection right now.

One example is a church-sponsored community service initiative in which people from all walks of life work together to restore a dilapidated park in the area. Everyone brings something different to the table, like gardening, painting, carpentry, or just serving refreshments. Some people are there to pray with and for the workers and the people in the area. Every act of service, no matter how small, is important for the bigger picture of healing and beauty, just like how each stone is important for building a temple. This not only helps the community but also helps the people involved grow emotionally and strengthens their friendships. This is what it means to live out our faith in real, powerful ways.

The different spiritual skills people have in the church are also very important for building and strengthening this temple. In 1 Corinthians 12, the Apostle Paul talks about the gifts of the Spirit. He stresses that these gifts are given for the good of all, to help each other and to advance God's Kingdom. You can teach, prophesy, heal, run the church, or be a gracious host. All of these gifts are important for the spiritual health and growth of the church community.

But why does this matter? Why is our active participation as living stones essential? Each time we use our gifts and serve, we are doing more than performing a task—we are obeying God's call to love one another and embody the teachings of Christ. This obedience promotes personal growth and has a ripple effect, encouraging and inspiring others to explore and use their gifts in service to God and each other.

Here, you have to consider the massive impact that could be realized globally if each person of faith were to live out their beliefs with undeterred commitment and a clear sense of purpose. Take a moment and consider a community where every individual's conduct is a reflection of Christ's love and promotes the spiritual advancement of others. Such a community has the potential to be a catalyst for transformative change. This is not merely a fanciful idea but rather the possible reality of the shared spiritual foundation we are constructing together.

Unity and Diversity in the Temple of God

The beautiful temple of God will be colored with the faith of every true believer, which will amalgamate into a cohesive design of our religion. When this diversity is coupled with the unity that binds us, it forms not just a structure but a masterpiece reflecting God's love and wisdom. The question arises, how, then, does the diversity of gifts and backgrounds among believers enhance the functionality and beauty of this spiritual temple? And how does the biblical call for unity manifest within this diverse body?

To answer the question, we need to draw insights from Paul's first letter to the Corinthians; we see a powerful illustration of how diversity in gifts serves the body of Christ. In 1 Corinthians 12:12-27, Paul compares the church to a human body where each part, no matter how seemingly insignificant, is central to the body's overall health and functionality. Just as the eye cannot say to the hand, "I have no need of you," neither can one believer deem another unnecessary. This diversity therein lies in the teaching, the encouragement, the hospitality, or even in the leadership. It is designed not to divide but to unify, making the church more resilient and effective in its mission.

Soup kitchens are a good example of a community project that needs a lot of different kinds of people to bring their own skills and knowledge to the table. The organizers are in charge of ensuring that everyone on the team works together as a single unit and that the kitchen runs smoothly. The cooks are the ones who make the food.

They use their knowledge of cooking to make tasty, healthy meals for everyone who comes to the kitchen. Servers are very important because they bring food to the guests, make sure everyone is fed, and keep the kitchen running smoothly. The people who clean up after meals are very important for keeping the kitchen clean and germ-free. Lastly, people who are willing to listen are very important for helping people who are having a hard time feeling better.

In the same way, each believer in a spiritual temple has a gift that is important for the church's growth and its purpose in the world. The church works well as a whole because each person brings their own special skills and gifts to the table. Some people may be divinely inspired to teach, while others may be inspired to speak or spread the gospel.

There are people who are gifted at running things, and there are people who are gifted at encouraging or merciful. Each of these gifts is important for ensuring the church runs smoothly, and its goal is carried out well. Churches can make a big difference in the world if they work together and use the skills that each believer has.

But what about unity? In the book *Life Together* by Dietrich Bonhoeffer, the author expands on the Christian community's life. They put high emphasis on how our unity derives from Christ and not mere human compatibility. Bonhoeffer writes, "Christian brotherhood is not an ideal which we must realize; it is rather a reality created by God in Christ in which we may participate." This participation requires humility, patience, and love—qualities that enable believers to live in harmony despite differences.

In practice, unity means prioritizing the collective mission over individual preferences. It involves making compromises, sometimes setting aside personal desires for the greater good of the community. It's about looking beyond ethnic, social, and economic differences to see the image of God in every believer. Unity in diversity means celebrating each unique attribute that each member brings to the table while working towards the same goal—glorifying God and advancing His kingdom.

How, then, can we live out this unity and diversity in our daily lives? Are we willing to embrace and encourage the diverse gifts within our church community? Do we strive to maintain the unity of the Spirit through the bond of peace, as urged in Ephesians 4:3?

We need to introspect here to be able to answer these questions. We need to strive to be builders of this spiritual temple, where diversity is not just tolerated but celebrated as essential, and unity is not enforced but incorporated as our strength. Let *this* be our commitment: to live out our faith with such genuine love and unity that the world will see and know Christ through us. Isn't this the ultimate witness to the power of the Gospel? Isn't this what it means to truly be the temple of God?

The Indwelling Presence of the Holy Spirit

The indwelling of the Holy Spirit in the life of a believer is considered to be a highly transformative experience that activates and completes the temple of God on earth. As the ultimate craftsman, the Holy Spirit doesn't just make minor adjustments; He fundamentally renovates our inner being to become a fitting residence for God Himself.

What does this truly mean for us? How does this transformation manifest in our lives and communities?

When the Holy Spirit descends upon a believer, it marks the beginning of a new existence. This divine presence within us is not just a passive occupancy but an active engagement and empowerment that changes everything. The Scriptures say in 1 Corinthians 3:16, *"Do you not know that you are God's temple and that God's Spirit dwells in you?"* This reality transforms believers into sacred spaces where the divine meets the mundane.

For people whose lives have been ruined by addiction and who are having a hard time finding any kind of hope; for these people, the Holy Spirit changes everything about their lives. Not only do I see a change in how they act, but I also see a change in who they are. They begin to see themselves not as slaves to their habits but as loved, valuable, and given the power to beat them by God. They are able to break free from addiction with the help of the Holy Spirit. They not only get sober, but they also find a new path that is full of purpose and meaning. That's the power of the Holy Spirit at work, changing people and whole communities.

This gift from the Holy Spirit isn't just for personal growth; it's for making the group stronger as a whole. Everyone who follows Christ gets stronger together. The Spirit gives gifts like prophecy, teaching, encouragement, and generosity to God's people. These gifts help the church serve better and bring unity and growth. For the Holy Spirit, these gifts are like tools that are made to meet the needs of the community and spread the Gospel.

We should ask ourselves if we're ready for the Holy Spirit to work in our lives. He wants to fill us, change us, and work through us. Or do we refuse to change because we are stuck in old habits and comforts?

Each person in a church would be fully filled with the power of the Holy Spirit. This kind of society would be full of love, peace, and divine power. It would be a sign of God's kingdom at work and a source of hope in a turbulent world. This is how God sees His temple and His people—a beautiful and difficult picture.

We need to be open to the Holy Spirit's direction as we think about how He lives inside us. Don't put out the fire of the Spirit. Instead, let it burn brightly inside us and change us from the inside out so that the world can meet the living God through us. To be the house of God means to bring His presence, power, and love to everyone we meet. What are you going to do today to let the Holy Spirit work through you? This should be our deepest thought, daily task, and greatest happiness.

Living as the Completed Temple

Living as part of the completed temple of God is a profound calling that extends far beyond Sunday worship; it permeates every aspect of our lives, influencing our relationships, our service, and our mission in the world. But what does it truly mean to embody the reality of the spiritual temple daily? How does this spiritual identity transform our interactions and engagements with the world around us?

Every deed, word, and thought has weight when we see ourselves as living temples where God's Spirit lives. We are not just ordinary people going through the hard parts of life; we are holy vessels that bring the presence of God into every space we enter. Realizing this can completely change how we act in our daily lives. Take the example of a believer who works in a high-stress business setting where aggressive behavior and self-promotion are normal. Because this person is a live temple, they are expected to be more honest and kind, showing God's light and truth in a place where people usually value the opposite.

Relationships are also severely affected by living in the temple. Rather than passing judgment, it exhorts us to extend grace, love unrestricted, and forgive those who have harmed us. Envision a family where conflicts and misunderstandings are causing strain. One who believes in this family, which is a functioning temple, is given the strength to be a peacemaker, to embody empathy and patience, and to initiate reconciliation.

They show the world the transforming power of God's presence by taking action that helps the family heal and restore.

Serving others also becomes a form of worship for us. Through acts of service such as mentoring children, helping at a local shelter, or supporting a community initiative, the holiness of the temple is extended beyond our church building into the community and the world at large. The seeds of faith and love planted by acts of service and kindness have the potential to bear fruit that endures forever. Take, for example, a congregation of Christians who band together to build or repair houses for the poor. With every brushstroke and hammer stroke, the church becomes more than a building; it becomes a community of servants, sharing the love and compassion of God with all who live in it.

And what about our mission in the world? Living as the completed temple compels us to spread the message of Jesus' love and salvation to all corners of the earth. This mission is not carried out by force or coercion but through lives so transformed by God's presence that others are drawn to Him. Each interaction, whether at home, in the workplace, or across seas in missions, becomes an opportunity to testify to the life-changing reality of knowing Jesus.

Here, we need to reflect: Are we truly living as temples of the Holy Spirit? How are our lives testifying to the sanctity and compassion that should characterize God's temple? Are we intentional about allowing God's Spirit to work through us, touching lives and transforming our environments?

The weight of this truth settles upon us. We are not merely collections of flesh and bone but vessels chosen to house the divine presence. This is not a casual designation but a solemn calling. It beckons us to rise above the shallow pursuits of the world and live with purpose.

This purpose demands authenticity. We cannot compartmentalize our faith, relegating it to Sundays or moments of crisis. It must permeate every facet of our existence, from the boardroom to the checkout line. Our actions become a reflection of the God who dwells within, a testament to His love and truth.

Living for ourselves becomes a distant memory. We are converted into sanctuaries, radiating God's light into a world often shrouded in darkness. The responsibility is weighty, the task demanding. Yet, within this challenge lies a significant privilege. We are entrusted with the power to touch lives, to offer solace and hope in the face of despair.

The question still lingers: How will we answer this call? It requires deep introspection and a ruthless examination of our priorities. Are we truly vessels worthy of housing the divine? Do our actions reflect the God we claim to serve?

This is not a call for empty piety or outward displays of devotion. It is a call to integrity, to a life lived in unwavering commitment to the highest good. It is a challenge to constantly refine ourselves, to become ever more worthy vessels of God's grace.

The path will not be easy. There will be moments of doubt, of temptation to stray. But let us remember the awesome power entrusted to us. We are living temples, and the world desperately needs the light we carry within. Let us rise to the occasion, not with fanfare, but with a quiet determination to honor the sacred calling we have received.

We are indeed vessels of the divine, called to embody His presence in every moment of our lives. This sacred calling challenges us to transcend the mundane, to infuse divine love and grace into our daily interactions, and to serve with a heart that reflects God's compassion. May we each rise to this calling with renewed commitment and fervor, understanding that every act of kindness, every word of truth, and every gesture of love is a brick in the spiritual edifice we are building together.

Let us live not just for today but for eternity as living testimonies of God's transformative power and love.

Chapter 8: The Temple of God Completion

"Then God blessed the seventh day and made it holy because on it he rested from all the work of creating that he had done."

-Genesis 2:3

The Bible whispers many secrets to us. All of these include an undying truth that chills me to the bone and sets my heart ablaze at the same time. It tells us we're not just bystanders in this grand story of faith. We're not just cheering from the sidelines. We are, in fact, the core building blocks, the living stones being fitted together to form a magnificent temple – God's temple.

Think about it. Look at Jesus's life, how he walked the earth, and every action as a brushstroke on the blueprint of this divine structure. His love, his sacrifice, his very resurrection—these are the cornerstones that hold everything together. And guess what? We get to be a part of that.

Being a follower of Christ isn't a spectator sport. It's a call to action, an invitation to roll up our sleeves and get to work. Continuing that legacy and contributing our individual stones to the temple walls is an enormous duty that has been placed upon us. It's more about making a positive impact than winning. Kindness, silent prayer, and loving choices are the cement that holds us together, strengthening and beautifying the temple.

But let me be honest, it's not always easy. There will be days when doubt creeps in, days when the weight of this calling feels heavy. But then I remember the completion. The Bible tells us this temple isn't some temporary structure destined to crumble. It's an eternal masterpiece, a testament to God's love that will stand forever. And to be a part of that, to know that even the smallest act of faith contributes to its glory – that's a privilege that takes my breath away.

So yes, the weight is heavy, and the responsibility is immense. But the reward?

The chance to be a living stone in God's eternal temple? That's a reason to rise each morning with a heart full of purpose and a spirit ready to build. We are not bystanders; we are the builders.

Understanding the Spiritual Temple in Scripture

Have you ever felt lost? Adrift in a sea of uncertainty, where you are desperately searching for a place to belong, a purpose that sets your soul on fire? The world throws so much at us – noise, doubt, a hollowness that nothing seems to fill. Nevertheless, I stand before you today with a truth that will crack open your hearts and flood them with light: we are not meant to wander alone! The Bible whispers a glorious secret: that we, the believers, are the living stones of a magnificent temple, God's holy dwelling place here on earth!

Take a moment to reflect on the majestic temple that stood in Jerusalem, serving as a symbol of God's presence for humankind. Imagine now something much more deep - a society bound together by faith, a temple not constructed of stone but of pounding hearts. That is the impact of the teachings found in the New Testament! Proverbs and scriptures like 1 Corinthians 3:16–17 remind us that we are dwelling places of the Holy Spirit.

God will destroy anyone who desecrates his temple because you are holy, like God's temple.

My friends, these words have more than one meaning. They're an enticement to live a life full of meaning and purpose, a rallying cry! The effect we could achieve is quite remarkable. Think about Sarah, the single mother who is both worn out and resolute as she works two jobs. She prays quietly for her children each night as she kneels by her bed. Sarah, your presence is like a beacon of light; you inspire a world that is in dire need of optimism and resilience.

Another example is Michael, a timid adolescent who, despite the difficulty, chooses to be kind and stands up to bullies. You are a living stone, Michael, laying the groundwork for compassion and reflecting God's love. A brick is set in the temple wall for every act of faith and every choice made with love. In this magnificent tale of trust, we do not merely observe.

We need to be honest here. The path we wish to walk won't always be smooth. There will be days when doubt creeps in, days when the world's noise drowns out the whispers of our hearts. We might question, "Am I good enough? Am I worthy of being a part of something this incredible?"

That's where the beauty of the temple metaphor comes in. It's not about our individual perfection. It's about the collective strength of the community we build together. We are all different shapes and sizes, with unique gifts and talents. But when we come together, united by our faith, something remarkable happens. We become a masterpiece, a testament to God's plan from creation to sanctification.

When we see the magnificent stained-glass windows in a cathedral, we see that each piece of colored glass is beautiful on its own, but when they come together, they create a breathtaking tapestry of light and story. That's the power of the spiritual temple! Each of us, with our flaws and imperfections, contributes to the breathtaking beauty of the whole.

So, here we halt and ponder questions like, will you be a living stone, a beacon of hope in a world that so desperately needs it? Don't let fear or doubt hold you back. Embrace the sacred responsibility, the privilege of being a part of something bigger than yourself. Together, let's build a temple that will stand the test of time. It shows that God's love echoes through eternity. Open your hearts, brothers, and sisters, and step into the glorious purpose that awaits!

Christ's Role in the Temple's Completion

The ministry of Jesus Christ on earth was not just about teaching or performing miracles—it was about laying the foundational stone for the spiritual temple, a temple not made with hands but within the hearts of believers. Through His actions and teachings, Jesus exemplified and initiated what would become the core structure of this divine temple. Every word He spoke, every deed He performed, was a brick in the construction of a spiritual edifice that would forever change the landscape of human spirituality.

Jesus' ministry beautifully modeled the qualities and functions of the temple. Consider the moment He declared in Luke 4:18-19, reading from Isaiah, that He came to "proclaim good news to the poor... to set the oppressed free." Here, Jesus aligns His mission with the temple's ultimate purpose: to be a place of refuge, healing, and proclamation of God's covenant. Every healing, every forgiveness of sins, and His tender mercies toward the marginalized were vivid demonstrations that God's presence had indeed broken into human experience in a tangible and transformative way.

However, the most notable aspect of Jesus' role in the temple's completion was His sacrificial death and triumphant resurrection. In John 2:19-21, Jesus spoke of destroying the temple and raising it in three days, alluding to His body as the temple. His death tore the veil in the Temple of Jerusalem from top to bottom, symbolizing the end of the old covenant and the inauguration of a new, living temple—His body, the church. This act laid the cornerstone of our faith, the bedrock upon which every believer stands.

His resurrection was the seal of approval on this new edifice. With Christ risen, the temple was not just restored but glorified, made eternal and accessible to all who would believe. Now, every believer becomes a living stone in this temple, called to continue the mission of Jesus, to embody His love, His mercy, and His truth.

When we think of a contemporary Christian who, motivated by the example that Christ set, extends her house to foster children, we are thinking of a modern-day believer. A living testimony to the power and presence of God in her life, each act of love and care that she provides is a true embodiment of the temple's purpose to shelter and nurture souls.

This prompts us to consider the following question: How do we embody the characteristics of the spiritual temple in our day-to-day lives? Are we, like Christ, a safe haven for those who are exhausted and a guiding light for those who have no hope? Does the way we conduct our lives announce freedom to those who are enslaved by different kinds of bonds?

It would be impossible to exaggerate the significance of this position. The act of living as a part of this finished temple is a serious and heavenly calling that requires us to be completely faithful and passionate about what we do. Because of this, we are challenged to rise beyond the mundane, to live out our faith with a profound sense of purpose and urgency, and to do so with the knowledge that the world comes into contact with the real God through us.

The Believer's Role in the Ongoing Construction

My fellow believers, have you ever felt like a mere brick adrift in a field of crumbling debris? Lost in a sea of unfulfilled potential, haunted by the ghosts of regret and uncertainty, you may ask what you could possibly bring to the table that could make a difference. A spiritual temple, a majestic house for God constructed from the souls of Christians, can seem intimidating, doesn't it? The first step toward being a living stone is to question everything and want to be a part of something greater than yourself.

In Ephesians 2:21-22, the Bible tells us, "In him, you also are being built together into a dwelling place for God in the Spirit." We are not just bricks waiting to be cemented into place. We are active participants in the ongoing construction of this temple.

Every choice we make, every battle we fight within ourselves, becomes a chisel, shaping us into the perfect piece for the divine structure.

For a person, let's say, someone who is fighting addiction, every day is a struggle, a fight for a moment of clarity. But if that person chooses to attend a support group, to seek help, to chip away at the walls their addiction has built around them. Their journey may be long, but every step you take strengthens the foundation of the temple.

Now, some might ask, "What about the quiet moments, the prayers whispered in the dark, the acts of kindness done when no one is watching?" Don't underestimate the power of those silent contributions, friends! They are the mortar that binds us together, the invisible threads that weave us into a tapestry of faith.

Our personal growth isn't just about self-improvement, though that's important too. It's about becoming the best version of ourselves so we can better serve the community—the living stones around us. We are called to encourage, to uplift, to be a shoulder to cry on, and a hand to hold.

But the responsibility doesn't stop there. Just like a physical temple needs constant care, the spiritual temple requires our vigilance. We must be the guardians against negativity, the weeders who uproot doubt and negativity that threatens to weaken the foundation.

The temple thrives on communal activities and shared experiences of faith. Imagine a group of volunteers at a soup kitchen, strangers brought together by a common purpose. They may come from different walks of life, but within the walls of that kitchen, they are united. They are building the temple, brick by brick, with every warm meal served and every kind word exchanged.

So, my friends, let us not be passive participants in this grand construction project. Let us embrace the challenge, the joy, and the immense responsibility of being living stones. Let us nurture our own spiritual growth, knowing that every step forward strengthens the temple's foundation. Let us be the guardians of light, weeding out negativity and offering unwavering support to our fellow stones.

Together, let us build a temple that resonates with God's love, a beacon of hope that will guide generations to come. Let our voices rise in unison, a chorus of faith that echoes through eternity. The world needs the strength, the compassion, the ever-gleaming light of the spiritual temple we are called to build. The question lingers no longer – will you answer the call? Will you be the living stone that completes the masterpiece? Let us rise together, brothers and sisters, and build a temple worthy of the divine presence it will house!

The Holy Spirit's Empowering Presence

The spiritual temple we are building can feel the same way at times. We, the living stones, come together, each with our unique gifts and passions. But how do we become more than a scattered collection? How do we transform into a unified masterpiece, a dwelling place worthy of God's presence?

The answer lies in the unseen hand of the Holy Spirit, the very essence of God himself, residing within each of us. It's like the missing piece of the mosaic puzzle, the element that brings everything together and infuses it with life. The Bible, in 1 Corinthians 3:16, tells us, *"Do you not know that you are God's temple and that the Spirit of God dwells in you?"*

This isn't some abstract concept. The Holy Spirit is the fire that ignites our faith, the sculptor who takes our rough edges and shapes us into vessels of light. Imagine Michael, the shy teenager we met before. Remember how he found the courage to stand up to bullies? That wasn't just Michael acting alone. It was the Holy Spirit empowering him, whispering strength in his ear, reminding him of the love that resides within him.

It is also the way the Holy Spirit operates. He points the way, encourages us to help others, and motivates us to share what we have with the world. We are not vying for recognition but rather working together to create something truly remarkable. Every one of us is essential to the whole, for we are Christ's body.

When we see a group of volunteers organizing a clothing drive, we see each person, empowered by the Holy Spirit, contribute their unique talent, and together, they create a haven of compassion and support.

The Holy Spirit doesn't shy away from the challenges we face within the temple walls either. He empowers us to confront negativity to weed out doubt and discord that threatens to weaken the structure. Remember John, the high school student who stood up to a bully? The Holy Spirit might nudge him to forgive the bully and offer kindness where there was once animosity. It's a tough call, but the Spirit empowers him to choose love, strengthening the foundation of compassion within the temple.

We should not be afraid to invite the Holy Spirit more fully into our lives. Let us be the clay, ready to be molded by the divine sculptor. Let us be the instruments, ready to be played by the heavenly musician. The Holy Spirit resides within each of us, waiting to empower, guide, and unite us in this glorious endeavor.

We need to build a temple that resonates with God's love, a beacon of unity that transcends our differences. Let our actions be a testament to the empowering presence of the Holy Spirit within us. The world needs the strength, the compassion, and the solid light of the spiritual temple we are called to build. The question lingers no longer – will you answer the call? Will you be the living stone that allows the Holy Spirit to complete the masterpiece? Open your hearts, brothers, and sisters, and let the divine transformation begin!

Living as a Completed Temple in the World

Not only is accepting that we are the finished temple of God a spiritual idea that should be celebrated in a church, but it should also be a fact that changes us and shows up in our daily lives. In a world that is often very different from these values, this heavenly calling pushes us to live with honesty, love, and holiness. But what does it really mean to live in this world? How does it affect how we treat each other, the choices we make, and our work in the world?

To begin, being honest when we serve the temple means that everything we say and do is in line with what Christ taught. It's about being honest and moral, even when lying might seem easier or more rewarding. Think about a businessman who works in a high-stakes setting where taking shortcuts is common. His decision to run his business honestly—by paying fair wages, turning down shady deals, and making sure all transactions are clear—becomes a strong sign of his faith. In this way, Christians shine a light on the right way to act and trust in a world where ethics aren't always clear.

One more thing that shows how to live as God's temple is love—love that is gentle, kind, and selfless. This kind of love, which is ready to go beyond limits and comfort zones, is like the selfless love of Christ. For example, think about the effect of Christians who volunteer to work in shelters for the homeless, not only serving food but also being friends, treating people with respect, and giving them honor. More than just meeting basic needs, these acts of love break down walls and build bridges, showing how Jesus loved everyone.

In a world filled with noise, a constant barrage of distractions that pull us away from the whispers of our hearts. The secular world can feel like a raging sea, threatening to drown out our connection to God. But there's a lifeline- a secret weapon for navigating these turbulent waters – prayer, meditation, scripture study- the sacred disciplines.

These aren't just dusty religious rituals, friends. They're lifelines to the source of our strength, the wellspring that quenches our thirst for purpose. Prayer isn't just about asking for things; it's a whispered conversation with the divine, a way to quiet the storm and hear the gentle guidance of the Holy Spirit.

Meditation isn't about emptying your mind; it's about focusing it, like a laser beam cutting through the fog of daily anxieties. It's a space to reconnect with yourself, to remember the sacred light that resides within you as a living stone in God's temple.

And scripture? It's not a dusty rulebook. It is a love letter from the Divine and a roadmap to navigate the complexities of life. Each verse is a brushstroke on the masterpiece of your faith, revealing the incredible potential that lies within you.

When practiced with intention, these disciplines become a shield against the world's negativity. They nourish your spirit, making you a beacon of hope in a world that desperately needs it. But the impact of your completed temple, of being a living stone filled with the Holy Spirit, extends far beyond personal fulfillment.

It's about becoming a living testament to God's love, a force for positive change in the world. Imagine the ripple effect of a life transformed by faith. You see an injustice, a gaping wound in the fabric of society – poverty, inequality, oppression. It ignites a fire within you, a burning desire to act.

It's about channeling the power of the Holy Spirit into transformative actions. Just like in Timothy Keller's book "Generous Justice," you understand your role as God's temple compels you to fight. You fight for the downtrodden, for a world where everyone has a chance to experience the love and grace you've received.

This isn't some distant dream, some far-off goal. It starts with you, right now, at this very moment. By nourishing your spirit through the sacred disciplines, you become a vessel overflowing with God's love. And that love, when shared through your actions, has the power to mend the broken world, one act of compassion at a time.

We need to open our hearts, brothers and sisters!!

Let the power of prayer, meditation, and scripture transform you. Become the living temple you were meant to be, a radiant beacon of hope in a world that desperately needs your light. Together, let's fulfill the mission of Christ, one act of love, one courageous stand for justice at a time. The world needs your completed temple, your overflowing cup of faith. Let's go change the world!

Living out this temple identity means that believers are actively involved in making the world a better place, reflecting God's kingdom on earth. Whether it's through advocating for fair policies, supporting educational initiatives, or participating in environmental stewardship, each action contributes to a global mission showcasing our faith's beauty and relevance.

Thus, as we consider our role as the completed temple in the world, let us ponder deeply: How are our lives preaching the gospel? Are our actions at work, at home, and in our communities reflecting the sanctity of the temple we embody?

Are we engaged in social issues with a heart of compassion and a mind for justice?

Embodying the temple of God is a profound and serious call. It challenges us to live out our faith with passion and sincerity, impacting every sphere of our existence and extending the love of Christ to every corner of the earth. Let this be our commitment, our lifestyle, and our witness—to live not just for ourselves but as vibrant sanctuaries of God's presence, demonstrating His love and truth to everyone we meet. How will you live out this sacred calling today?

Chapter 9: The Word Became Flesh

[19] "A little while longer and the world will see Me no more, but you will see Me. Because I live, you will live also."

- John 14:19

Meditation:

The more and more one meditates and looks at what God is saying to mankind, the more it is clear that he manifests his love, grace, mercy, and kindness into the world to save us. As Jesus was speaking to the early disciples and explaining in the best way possible the infinite truth that only God can convey to a soul, the disciples were still not quite sure of what Jesus was saying to them. A little while longer, the world will see ME no more. The World we live in today is not created by God. Yes, God created everything, yet he did not create this environment that we live in today. This World was created out of disobedience to God.

We need to look at things from another perspective. If one is given directions for baking cornbread a certain way yet disregards the instructions given and precedes doing it according to one's own knowledge, the bread will not come out the way it was originally intended to come out.

The bread will not come out the way it is intended because the person has not followed the specific instructions for baking the bread. So those people who are of the world, those people who do not follow the instructions of Jesus, live in this World. Those who live in this World cannot "See" Jesus. Those who continue to live under the Covenant of the first Kingdom of Adam and Eve can not "see" Jesus. This is the reason it is so important for us to get to know who we are in Christ Jesus. Although we are in this World, according to John 17:16, They are not of the world, just as I am not of the world.[1617] Sanctify them by Your truth. Your word is truth." Jesus was praying to God the Father for the disciples.

All who believe and follow Jesus and his work are indeed his disciples. So, as disciples of Jesus, the person is not part of this world. Jesus further states that because his disciples are not of this world, the world will see him no longer, but they will see him. I would like to reveal to you that as a disciple of Jesus, although you are in the World (TODAY), you are able to "see" Jesus. The World can not see Jesus, nor can they know Jesus, but as a disciple of Jesus, as a person who has a personal relationship with Jesus, that person is able to see Jesus through the "eyes" of his faith.

"Then the man and his wife heard the sound of the Lord God as he was walking in the garden in the cool of the day, and they hid from the Lord God among the trees of the garden."

- Genesis 3:8

In the shadows of the Garden of Eden, as recounted in Genesis 3:8, humanity first experienced separation from God. Adam and Eve, once in perfect communion with their Creator, hid themselves among the trees, their hearts heavy with the weight of disobedience. This poignant moment marks not just the physical distancing from God but a profound spiritual rift. It was here that the serene fabric of trust and intimacy was torn, ushering in an era of estrangement between God and man.

Centuries later, this chasm was addressed directly by the incarnation of Christ. Jesus, the Word made flesh, represents God's ultimate response to the disobedience that severed humanity from its divine source. In John 14:19, Jesus promises, *"A little while longer and the world will see Me no more, but you will see Me."* This promise underscores a pivotal reversal of that ancient separation. While the world, operating under the old covenant of law and transgression, could no longer perceive Him, those who embraced His new covenant of grace would indeed see Him, not just as a historical figure but as a present and living reality.

In Mere Christianity, C.S. Lewis eloquently discusses this notion of separation and reconciliation. He explains how the incarnation bridges the vast gap between God and humanity, offering a relationship restored not through human effort but through divine intervention. This intervention, Lewis suggests, is not merely a patch-up job but a profound restoration of what was intended before humanity's fall.

When we see a person estranged from their family due to past mistakes and misunderstandings, despite numerous attempts to mend the relationship, a deep-seated bitterness remains. When reconciliation finally occurs, it's often through an act of unconditional love or forgiveness, mirroring on a human level what Christ did on a divine scale. Just as this person's return to their family transforms the dynamics of their relationships, so too does Christ's presence transform those who accept Him.

The incarnation, then, is not just an event in history. It is the ongoing state of Jesus living among us, guiding, teaching, and loving us. It is God walking in the garden in the cool of the day, calling out to us, not content to let us remain hidden in our shame and sin. He comes close, He dwells within, and He restores.

This truth should deeply affect how we live as believers. Knowing that Christ has bridged the ultimate divide should inspire us to live openly and honestly before God, no longer hiding but approaching Him with confidence. It compels us to extend this same grace to others, actively working to bridge gaps of division and strife in our communities and relationships.

As we reflect on the incarnation as God's response to our disobedience, let us embrace our role in this ongoing narrative of redemption. Let us live as those who not only believe in but also visibly demonstrate the reality of God with us, Immanuel. How will you let the truth of Christ's presence influence your actions today? How will you show the world that, indeed, the separation has been countered and the presence of Christ is a reality in your life? Let these questions guide us as we continue to navigate our faith journey, propelled by the transformative power of the incarnation.

Visibility of Christ to Believers vs. the World

Being able to "see" Jesus, to really feel and understand His presence and message, sets a deep line between Christians and the rest of the world. This difference, which comes from faith, changes a person's spirituality and how believers interact with and affect the world outside of faith.

Believers don't see Jesus with their eyes; they have a spiritual insight, a deep understanding of His rule and His involvement in their lives. This openness is beautifully explored in Mere

Christianity by C.S. Lewis. In it, Lewis talks about the difference between knowing about God intellectually and really understanding God through a strong, living faith. He says that coming to see Jesus is like turning on a light in a dark room. The truth was always there, but without Christ's light, it can't be seen, felt, or understood.

Think about the life of a young woman who lives in a busy city. She is surrounded by modern stresses and distractions that can make it hard to focus on the spiritual. In her view, Jesus could be just another historical person or a faraway religious icon, unlike other characters from ancient stories. But her world changes when she meets the living Christ through personal faith, like when she is in a very bad situation or when a friend tells her the truth. She starts to see Jesus everywhere—in the world's beauty, the kindness of strangers, and life's problems and difficulties. The fact that she can see Christ changes her once-boring daily life into a lively tapestry of spiritual encounters that keep her faith strong and guide her actions.

This view has a big impact on how Christians deal with the rest of society. Seeing Jesus frees people to live in a way that goes against cultural norms, often at odds with what the Bible says. They bring a sense of morality and a sense of purpose to their jobs, schools, and social groups that can be both interesting and convicting to those around them.

For instance, we see a businessman who sees Jesus in his daily life, who might choose honesty over a deal that would make him a lot of money, but it is also illegal. This would show his coworkers that honesty is more important than making money. A student who sees Jesus in the people she talks to might treat her peers from all walks of life with love and respect, going against the social rules of cliques and exclusion.

This visibility overpoweringly influences evangelism. Believers are called not just to see Jesus themselves but also to be mirrors reflecting His light to others. Their lives, transformed by this visibility, become testimonies to the truth and power of the Gospel. They live as beacons of hope in a hopeless world, drawing others not by forceful argument but by the compelling evidence of lives beautifully and radically changed.

Therefore, as we reflect on the spiritual implications of seeing Jesus, we must ask ourselves: How clear is our vision? Are we daily seeking to sharpen our spiritual sight through prayer, Scripture, and fellowship? How are we reflecting Christ's image to those who are still stumbling in the darkness?

This journey of faith is both a profound privilege and a serious responsibility. Let it be said of us that we lived not as those who merely glanced at Jesus but as those who gazed deeply, loved passionately, and followed closely. How will you let your sight of Jesus transform not just your life but also the lives of those around you today? Let this challenge stir us to deeper commitment and more vibrant faith.

The Role of Faith in Seeing Jesus

Have you ever felt like the world is shrouded in a thick fog? You reach out, searching for something solid to hold onto, but all you find is emptiness and doubt. The Bible tells us in John 14:19, *"A little while longer and the world will see Me no more, but you will see Me. Because I live, you will live also."* These words hold a promise, a beacon of light in the midst of confusion. But how do we, as believers, break through the fog and truly "see" Jesus?

The answer lies in faith, my friends. It's not a blind leap but a bridge that allows us to cross the chasm between the physical and spiritual realms. It's a lens that sharpens our vision, allowing us to perceive the fingerprints of God in the everyday moments of life.

Here, let us take the example of Sarah, who is a single mom. The world might see only struggle in her eyes, the weight of responsibility threatening to crush her. But Sarah has faith. She sees Jesus in the quiet moments of prayer, in the unexpected kindness of a stranger, and in the strength she finds to keep going for her children. Her faith allows her to "see" Jesus, not with her physical eyes, but with the eyes of her heart.

Faith isn't always sunshine and rainbows, though. There will be times when the fog thickens when doubt creeps in like a thief in the night. The world, with its relentless noise and negativity, can make it hard to hold onto those precious glimpses of Jesus. We see suffering, injustice, and pain, and it can shake our faith to its core.

Or, let's consider the story of a shy teenager who found the courage to stand up to bullies. The world might mock him and call him naive for believing in something they can't see. But he has a secret weapon – his faith. He "sees" Jesus in the act of standing up for what's right, even when it's hard. He finds strength in the knowledge that Jesus himself faced rejection and persecution.

The question here arises: how do we strengthen our faith in the face of these challenges?

You see, it is a two-way road that we will "see" him. Just like any relationship, our faith in Christ needs nurturing.

If we look at a neglected garden, we see nothing but thorns and weeds that will take over if left untended. But with careful attention, regular watering, and weeding, beautiful flowers will bloom. It's the same with faith. We need to spend time in prayer, scripture study, and surrounding ourselves with other believers. These are the tools that help us cultivate and strengthen our faith.

And as our faith grows, so does our ability to "see" Jesus in the world around us. We see him in the breathtaking beauty of nature, in the resilience of the human spirit, in the acts of kindness, big or small, that touch our lives every day.

The world might be skeptical, but that shouldn't deter us. Remember John 17:16, *"They are not of the world, just as I am not of the world."* We are not called to blend in with the fog. We are called to be beacons of light, living testimonies to the transformative power of faith.

We need to open our hearts, brothers and sisters.

Let faith be the lens through which you view the world. Let it be the bridge that allows you to "see" Jesus in every aspect of your life. The world needs your unwavering faith, your unwavering belief in the presence of Christ. Together, let's pierce the fog with the light of our faith, illuminating the path for ourselves and for those around us. Remember, the promise is true: "Because I live, you will live also." Let's live a life that reflects that promise, a life where we see Jesus not just in the future but in every precious moment, right here, right now.

Future Implications of the Incarnation

The incarnation of Christ—God-made flesh—stands as a cornerstone of Christian theology, rich with implications not just for the past or present but for the future of the church and the world. As we move forward in a rapidly changing society, where technological advances and shifts in societal values continually reshape our landscape, the incarnation remains a profound, unchanging truth with the power to speak into these evolutions.

One might consider Philip Yancey's "The Jesus I Never Knew" for a deeper understanding of how the radical nature of Christ's earthly life and ministry continues to challenge and inspire believers across ages. Yancey unpacks the dynamic and sometimes counterintuitive teachings of Jesus, showing how they cut across cultural and temporal boundaries to offer timeless insights into human behavior and divine expectations.

Theologically, the ongoing academic and spiritual study of what it means for Christ to become human leads to a deeper understanding of what it means to be human in relation to the divine. These philosophical inquiries become more important as our world dives deeper into the fields of artificial intelligence and genetic engineering. They help set the stage for important moral conversations and show the church how to answer questions about people, creation, and the moral effects of new technologies.

When looking at society as a whole, the incarnation provides a very different story as nations become more diverse and secular ideas become more popular. It talks about a God who is not far away or uninterested but who has a face, a name, and a touch. This truth pushes the church to keep a strong, relational view of faith that goes beyond rules or rituals and instead gives a relationship that changes people.

Take a look at a real-life example of a community project that uses cutting-edge technology to meet social needs. For example, AI could be used to help poor areas get more food. Here, Christians can bring the incarnational principle of service and presence to bear, making sure that the worth and dignity of each person are preserved even as technology is used. This shows how Jesus' mission as a human being never forgot about the one person among many.

Then the question arises: how does the church communicate and embody the truth of Christ's presence in such a diverse and complex environment? It is imminently crucial. The methods may evolve—leveraging digital platforms, engaging in virtual reality spaces, or utilizing social media—but the message of a God who became man to redeem mankind must remain clear and compelling. The church must become adept at articulating this profound mystery in ways that resonate with contemporary ears yet remain firmly rooted in scriptural truth.

Speculating on the future implications of the incarnation, it is essential to consider our role in this unfolding story. Are we, as modern-day disciples, ready to live out and communicate this significant truth with courage and creativity? How can we ensure that our ministries and individual lives reflect the incarnational reality that God is with us, not just in history, but here and now, in every future moment we are given?

The challenge for believers is not just to hold to the truth of the incarnation but to actively demonstrate its relevance and power. This involves a deep commitment to understanding the times, engaging with love and wisdom, and embodying Christ's presence in every interaction—be it digital or face-to-face. As we move forward, let us carry this sacred responsibility with humility and passion, inspired by the God who stepped into time for us, ensuring that His life-giving presence is felt in every corner of our evolving world.

www.ingramcontent.com/pod-product-compliance
Lightning Source LLC
Chambersburg PA
CBHW072012150726
47999CB00002B/619